Keep Your Kids Straight

What Parents Need to Know about Drugs and Alcohol

Ronald C.
Main, Ph.D.
and
Judy
Zervas, C.D.C.

Human Services Institute
Bradenton

FIRST EDITION
SECOND PRINTING

Produced by Book Creations, Inc.
Lyle Kenyon Engel. Founder

Library of Congress Cataloging-in-Publication Data

Main, Ronald C.
     Keep your kids straight : what parents need to know about drugs
and alcohol / by Ronald C. Main and Judy Zervas.
        p.   cm.
     Includes bibliographical references and index.
     ISBN 0-8306-7681-3
     1. Teenagers—United States—Drug use. 2. Teenagers—United
States—Alcohol use.   3. Drug abuse—United States—Prevention.
4. Alcoholism—United States—Prevention.   5. Child rearing—United
States.   I. Zervas, Judy.   II. Title.
HV5824.Y68M353   1991
649'.4—dc20   90-21674
                                                                          CIP

TAB Books offers software for sale. For information and a catalog,
please contact TAB Software Department, Blue Ridge Summit,
PA 17294-0850.

Questions regarding the content of this book should be addressed to:

Reader Inquiry Branch
TAB Books
Blue Ridge Summit, PA 17294-0850

Acquisitions Editor: Kimberly Tabor
Development Editor: Lee Marvin Joinder, Ph.D.
Copy Editor: Pat Hammond
Cover photograph: Susan Riley, Harrisonburg, VA
Cover Design: Lori E. Schlosser

Contents

Preface

As a principal in charge of student discipline and as a chemical dependency counselor in the same high school for almost a decade, we have worked with hundreds of students who have become involved with substance abuse. They have run the gamut from first time experimenters to hard core abusers. We found a common thread running through almost all of their families—a lack of accurate information about teenage alcohol and drug use. The parents consistently admitted that they were naive and ill-informed.

"If only I had known" is one of the most heartwrenching statements the parent of an abusing teenager can make. Inevitably parents feel that they have failed and as they learn that there were helpful steps which they could have taken, the burden of guilt becomes enormous. They never knew about low-key confrontation, negotiating a contract, getting a sincere commitment, how to arrange an evaluation, or when an intervention is appropriate. But mostly they had never learned the protective steps which should have been taken much earlier.

Unfortunately, the few parents who truly know the world of teenage alcohol and drug abuse are those who have lived through it. In examining books in libraries and bookstores dealing with teenage alcohol and drug abuse we found plenty of information about the scope and seriousness of the problem at the societal level, explanations of the nature of addiction, the difficulty of treatment, and many dramatic case studies. Missing were specific actions that parents could and should take and the options that are open to them.

This book is different. It reveals how to avoid the six most common mistakes parents make in their efforts to keep their kids straight.

- Neglecting to teach your children refusal skills
- Failing to recognize warning signs
- Overlooking signs of abuse and avoiding confrontation
- Acting as enablers without realizing it
- Reacting with anger, threats and ultimatums
- Keeping the problem private; delaying outside help

The best defense against your child's becoming involved with substance abuse is being informed *before* a problem arises. Parental influence is the first and primary line of defense. This book is a step-by-step approach, giving important information and strategies for you to use at each phase of the problem—from preparing kids to face temptations through living with a determined substance abuser. Its chapters follow the classic progression of drug dependency.

The anecdotes and case histories are all true, taken from the personal experience of students and their families. Only the names and identifying details of the children and families have been changed to protect their privacy. Our suggestions for parents are not theoretical. They represent what parents with real life experiences think you should know and do to keep drugs from destroying your child's future.

How to Use This Book

We recommend that you read the entire book first. By doing this you will see the complete picture and all of the steps—each appropriate at certain points in the progression of drug abuse.

Chapter Three begins the sequence which becomes progressively more serious. It may be tempting to turn immediately to the chapter which you feel in most pertinent, and take action. But unless you know the beginnings, to insure that you have made an accurate diagnosis, and unless you know the subsequent phases, so that you can guage progression, you are limiting your effectiveness. After a complete reading you can return to the chapters which speak directly to your situation.

Use the book as a resource manual to help you plan your approach. A complete reading gives you the information you need to focus on the appropriate strategy. This is essential because your responses also follow a progression which grows increasingly more serious.

Keeping Your Kids Straight is intended to empower you with the knowledge you need to combat the negative forces your child will face while growing up. Many, many parents join us in wishing you success.

Chapter One

What You Don't Know
Can Hurt You

No parent can afford to be uninformed about the world of teenage alcohol and drug abuse. Relying on your children to build their own safeguards is too risky. Many pressures in our society make drugs and alcohol look very attractive to inexperienced youngsters; as a parent you need to understand those forces and counter them with appropriate actions. Please believe that your children will have opportunities, tempting opportunities, presented to them almost constantly. Unless you take every step that you can to prepare them, some of them may make the wrong choices out of ignorance and innocence.

The steps outlined in this book are not dramatic or difficult; they represent sound parenting behaviors plus some actions that are unique to the prevention of abuse. Parents who have suffered through teenage abuse are the source for this book's advice; many have learned, too late, what they should have known and what they should have done. At one time they had the same confidence that you probably feel right now—that none of your kids will ever get messed up with abuse. Those parents regret that misplaced confidence because it caused them to slide casually by the whole issue of teenage abuse and let their children fend for themselves. Some parents of pregnant teenagers have made a similar mistake.

The campaign to keep your children free of drug and alcohol abuse can be short and easy, or it can seem like World War III. You may be forced into a series of tactics that keep intensifying as the problem moves to more serious stages. You must work hard at prevention and protection but be prepared to handle experimentation and, if the problem persists and progresses, you must progress with it.

For a parent there is no giving up. Once your children reach the age of majority, your influence drops off dramatically. Until that time you must assume major responsibility.

HOW SCARED SHOULD YOU BE?

The following statistics are to remind you that every tally marked by these researchers represents somebody's child[1]:

- alcohol- and drug-related deaths are the number one killer of 15- to 24-year-olds

- recent surveys show that the first drinking experience occurs at around age 12

---

[1] Statistics from the *National Institute on Alcohol Abuse* and *The Search Institute* - see bibliography.

- over one-half of all junior high students used alcohol in the past year

- an estimated 3.3 million teenagers aged 14 to 17 are showing signs that they may develop serious alcohol-related problems

- among high school seniors 65% have used alcohol in the last month, 23% marijuana, 30% tobacco, and 6% cocaine

- 58% of high school seniors have used at least one illegal drug; 17% have tried cocaine

THE PROFIT PROMOTERS

Recent efforts by the alcohol industry to promote safe driving and responsible drinking are commendable. Unfortunately, their efforts hardly neutralize their enormous efforts to promote the drinking of alcoholic beverages. Some estimates put the annual advertising dollars spent on alcohol over the 400 million dollar mark; their advertisements are highly effective and frequently win awards within the media industry. Obviously they would not be happy if alcohol consumption dropped. We can be assured that they will continue to promote their product as one that goes hand-in-hand with glamour, good times, and success.

A second giant conglomerate is less open about its influence. It is the international network that supplies illegal drugs. To grasp the magnitude of their influence read *The Underground Empire* by James Mills, a frightening nonfiction account of a worldwide illegal industry. This quotation from his book describes the enormity of the profit motive: "The inhabitants of the earth spend more money on illegal drugs than they spend on food. More than they spend on housing, clothes, education, medical care, or any product or service." (Mills 1986,1)

This goliath eventually works its way into the streets, parks, shopping malls, and schools of nearly every community in this country. Its operatives generously supply their products to those on the fringes of society who, in turn, offer illegal drugs, often free, to the uninitiated. They are confident that samples given away will return high dividends; it's a sales gimmick that never seems to wear out.

We all know about the violence and ruthlessness that characterize this element of our population; they are engaged in a very profitable war. The Coast Guard, United States Customs officials, and federal, state and local narcotics agents have not been able to stop them; therefore, we can be assured that a supply of illegal drugs will always be available to our children.

IT'S A TOSS-UP

Illegal drug abuse or alcohol abuse: which is worse for a teenager? A case can be made either way. The use of alcohol so permeates our society that its devastation is often overlooked. For years our culture portrayed drunkenness, in movies and television, as a comic device. Drunks appeared as amusing, rubber-legged, bleary-eyed, slurry-voiced characters who said and did outrageous things. One nightclub comedian made a living by imitating a drunk; it was the basis for his entire act. For years the host of the *Tonight Show*, a television favorite, made a long-running joke out of his sidekick's drinking capacity. But drunkenness is no longer a laughing matter, and the comedy is wearing thin.

The vast majority of Americans, eighty percent or more, drink socially; of that number, ten to fifteen percent have drinking problems. Since most of us can drink without serious danger, we are more willing to accept some alcohol experimentation by youngsters. Because of this familiarity, we tend to classify alcohol as less threatening than the unknown world of illegal drugs. By any standard, though, alcohol is the most destructive drug in our country. It has started over three million teenagers down the abuse pathway.

For a young person, alcohol as the drug of choice has many advantages. It is inexpensive, sealed and certified by a regulated industry, commonplace, and easily available at retail outlets to anyone of age or anyone with access to a phony driver's license. A common practice of some young people is to wait in a liquor store parking lot for an adult who is willing to go in and buy them some liquor. Sometimes it's even older brothers or sisters who will do the buying.

Illegal drugs are more sinister than alcohol. They are unfamiliar and frightening to most of us. They frequently come from foreign lands, carry no standards of sanitation or content, and are distributed illegally by the most unsavory element of our population—criminals. No wonder we're scared.

In this book, abuse is abuse—whether it's alcohol or illegal drugs. Both are our enemies, and the tactics we use against them are nearly the same. Our ideal goal for our children is that they abstain from both alcohol and drugs, because without a beginning there can be no progression. A major reason is the very real danger of serious addiction. Following is a scientific, but frightening, account of the seductive power of one popular street drug, cocaine.

A MONKEY'S TALE

As part of a laboratory experiment, scientists implanted rhesus monkeys with an intravenous tube leading to a major vein in their bodies. When the monkeys pushed a certain lever in their specially equipped cage, they would receive a measured dose of cocaine. Here are the results of some experiments:

1. Once having learned the connection between the lever and the cocaine, monkeys were willing to press the lever over six thousand times for a single injection. Some went over twelve thousand.

2. When given a choice between cocaine and food, the monkeys chose cocaine to the point of starvation.

3. When given a choice between a lever yielding a large dose of cocaine and a painful electrical shock, or a lever yielding a small dose of cocaine but no electrical shock, the monkeys chose large doses with the painful shock.

4. When given unlimited access to the cage and the cocaine, monkeys sometimes ingested doses large enough to produce convulsions that can lead to death.

Until about 1986 cocaine was expensive and the domain of the wealthy—a so-called "chic" drug. Now it is out on the streets, much reduced in price, and available in many forms to teenagers. It may be replacing marijuana as the young people's drug of choice.

BUT MY KIDS ARE SPECIAL!

Yes, your kids are special; that is why you owe them the best protection that you can provide. Being special, however, isn't enough. Statistics guarantee that some of our children will become victims. What we don't know is which ones—because abusers don't run to type.

Abuse is nondiscriminatory. It crosses all lines: race, religion, nationality, sex, intelligence, social status, talent, popularity, family background—and every differential you can imagine. Below are descriptions of a panel of youngsters, all abusers and treatment center veterans, who recently addressed a high school assembly program. Their profiles are brief, but they illustrate the variety of kids who succumb to abuse:

Nancy - free spirit, brilliant student, active in church youth organizations; a wealthy, aggressive, twice-divorced mother

Andy - learning disabled, a loner, rigid personality, strong self-esteem; working-class parents who are abstainers

Matt - average ability but very low achiever, low key, passive, potential dropout, poor self-esteem; alcoholic father, warm and loving mother

Jimmy - handsome, near genius, fierce home pressure for achievement, attracted to offbeat companions and causes, strong self-discipline; fundamentalist parents

Susie - bright, popular with all students, tries to take care of everyone else, great empathizer, very low self-esteem; from heavy-drinking, highly sociable, and successful family

Jennifer - average scholastic ability but hopelessly behind in class, hostile, angry, aggressive, in constant fights and arguments at school and home; supportive but bewildered parents who provide a stable home life

These seven youngsters, all under 18 years of age, are a typical cross section of teenage abusers; they had almost nothing in common until they became abusers. Now they have these things in common:

- All knew they were breaking the law as well as family rules.

- All believed they would never have any trouble handling alcohol or drugs.

- All followed the classic progression for youngsters —tobacco, beer, stronger liquors, drugs.

- All have been to juvenile court.

- All denied being abusers until the day they entered treatment.

- All are terrified that they will weaken and return to abuse—some pray for strength.

All began with casual, occasional use and progressed until they were bona fide abusers, spending most of their time and energy using, dealing, or planning how to use and deal. They may have started as naive and innocent kids but they all reached a level of use that overpowered them. They entered treatment because their lives were out of control and they knew it.

They are all examples of the progressive nature of abuse. *The National Institute of Alcohol Abuse* describes the decision by a youngster to drink as a critical turning point. Their findings show that while abstainers seem insulated against other common teenage problem behaviors, both alcohol and cigarette use are often gateways to drug use and further problems. Once begun, the outcome of this progression is a dangerous gamble. Many treatment centers follow the lead of the *American Medical Association* in classifying alcoholism as a progressive disease that, unless treated, is fatal.

None of these youngsters, all struggling to stay clean, could have received a preventive vaccine; none exists. No screening device would have predicted in advance that they would become victims. None of the adults who knew them as young children saw telltale signs that would have marked them as vulnerable. Yet each of them fell into the trap of teenage abuse. Your children will face the same temptations that these seven faced. You can't shield them from exposure to alcohol and drugs any more than you can shield them from cigarettes and soft drinks; it can't be done.

THE RESIDUE OF TEENAGE ABUSE

Still unknown to these seven is the full measure of what they have missed. All characterize their teenage years as dominated by abuse—part of the time with their senses dulled or distorted by booze or drugs, and part of it scurrying and scrambling to both supply and conceal a growing dependency. They had little time for normal development during one of life's most crucial periods—the passage from child to adult.

Adolescence is the key time for learning coping techniques. The excitement of youth heightens each success and failure; working through the highs and lows is part of the maturing process. Coping via mood-altering substances allows a youngster to neutralize the problems of living a normal life. The teenager can hold them at arm's length so that he or she never has to come to terms with them. Abuse distorts reality. It arrests the maturation process at the critical stage of adolescence, so abusers never have a chance to develop; they carry a psychological deficit forever.

Something important for adolescents to learn is the fact that today's disaster doesn't mean the sun won't come out tomorrow. They learn to survive the disappointment, to live with the temporary pain and eventually bounce back. Thus they gradually gain the strength to live through larger disappointment and build the self-confidence needed to handle life's problems. It's the way children grow up.

HOW HIGH ARE THE STAKES?

The stakes are as high as life itself. If that sounds over-dramatic, so be it. We KNOW that alcohol- and drug-related accidents are the leading cause of death in the age group of fifteen to twenty-four. We KNOW that chemical abuse is present in one-half of teenage suicides, and that the number of suicides increases each year.

Are those stakes high enough?

How about the other fringe benefits of teenage chemical abuse? What happens to families who battle for years with a teenager turned nasty and uncooperative because of abuse? What happens to harmony, to brothers and sisters, to economic resources depleted by treatment costs, to emotional scars, to the haunting guilt and broken hearts of parents? Abuse is a leech that sucks the happiness out of life.

What happens to the victim?

- *despair and depression, talent wasted, potential unrealized, and absolutely no sense of self-worth*

Has there ever been a recovering abuser who is glad that he or she began? Of course not! Has there ever been a beginner who believed that he or she would become an abuser? Of course not!

The stakes are far too high and the odds are too great!

DAVE'S CASE

This is a true story of a family that seemed to do all the right things and still fell victim to abuse. Dave had parents who would make an adoption agency beam. His father was an insurance executive and a church deacon; his mother, a registered nurse. The family values seemed solid as a rock, with alcohol and drugs nowhere in the life of the family—until Dave hit junior high school. David was an innately bright student who had always learned easily, but his grades began to slip—from As and Bs to Cs and Ds. Athletics, a long-time source of excitement and success for him, became less important; both interest and performance began to lag. His personality—outgoing, affable, friendly, and charming—was no longer consistent. His delightful ability to be silly and make everyone else silly seemed to disappear.

Although his parents puzzled and agonized over these changes, they felt that Dave was a good kid, so they remained patient, kept faith in him, tried to keep communications open, believed his explanations even when they sounded shaky, and waited for him to find his way. He never found it.

In three years Dave progressed from beer blasts to hard liquor to marijuana smoking to pills, both uppers and downers, and dropping acid. Often he mixed his usage; that practice finally put him into treatment. One summer evening at a party while drinking and smoking pot he also dropped acid. The combination triggered convulsions. Alarmed, his friends had sense enough to call the police, who took Dave to a detox center. When he recovered, he asked his parents to send him to treatment. He knew that he had lost control of his life.

He spent six months in a residential treatment center. His usage had become so heavy that his parents were astonished when, as part of his treatment, he related his complete drug history to them. The astonishment of his parents was not a facade; it was genuine. Dave had been an ingenious user because he knew that he was violating family values; secrecy was paramount. He made certain that his parents never saw him high or discovered any physical evidence of his assortment of substances. His explanations were imaginative, and he exploited to the maximum the trust that his parents had in him. His guilt from this life of deceit was enormous and was a major factor in his requesting treatment.

The parents felt like failures and fools. They had not read the secondary signals—the declining grades, changing interests, new friends, and altered personality—as connected to abuse. They assumed Dave was struggling through a particularly rough period of adolescence, rougher than their other children had experienced.

This story has not ended. As of this writing, Dave has graduated from high school—just barely—and is hoping to attend college. The prognosis is not bright. He has trouble concentrating on tasks, deep bouts of depression, and severe headaches, and his personality is uneven. There are some periods when he can be his old charming self and others when self-doubt, anxiety, and frustration take over. He has had several short relapses of abuse.

His parents continue to stand by him with their love and support but believe that their real Dave will never return, that part of him has been damaged beyond repair. They suspect that his intellect, once so bright, is now permanently dimmed.

They don't understand why he started, why he continued, and why someone, including themselves, didn't realize what Dave was doing to himself and stop him in time.

A WINNING PROFILE

Some data suggest that kids who stay free of drugs and alcohol also have some things in common. From an Iowa study of high school students, those who did not use shared several tendencies, including those listed below:

- They have friends who also abstain and do not approve of drugs and alcohol.

- They are involved in church and extracurricular activities.

- They spend free time at home, school, or church.

- They share affection often with parents.

- They communicate well with parents.

- They have received firm guidelines about alcohol and drugs from their parents.

- They earn better than average grades.

- They do not smoke or chew tobacco.

- They have parents who do not use tobacco or alcohol.

Please notice that four of those nine categories involve the behavior of the parents.

Chapter Two

Why Do Kids Start ?

Parents often wonder why their children ever got started using; they are often totally bewildered. Behavioral psychologists maintain that most human beings make choices that they think will bring them the most satisfaction. It makes sense, then, to look at the motivation that leads adolescents to drugs and alcohol as a source of satisfaction. The most common reasons are a need to appear mature, to have a good time, to satisfy curiosity, to belong to a group, or to alleviate discomfort and pain.

FOLLOW THE LEADER

Both boys and girls often begin smoking cigarettes in early adolescence as a way of showing that they are more grown up than they seem. Interestingly enough, boys reserve cigars and pipes until later, when they want to announce that they are ready for full-fledged manhood. Teenagers often view alcohol in the same way—as an announcement of maturity. Kids can't help but notice the well-established custom of offering alcohol to guests to loosen them up and relieve the tension of social gatherings. They assume alcohol is a surefire route to a good time, so they imitate the adults. Street drugs, which were unfamiliar and frightening to older generations, have now become commonplace and serve as a substitute for or a supplement to alcohol.

CURIOSITY

Curiosity also has its role. Kids hear about 'trips,' incredible highs,' and 'unbelievable sensations,' and they want to give drugs a try. The accounts, often exaggerated, sound daring and exciting, and they have that lovely forbidden flavor. Why not "Go For It!"?

BELONGING

An even more common reason for using is a universal characteristic of teenage life called peer pressure. Volumes have been written about the struggle for acceptance that torments teenagers. The pressure to belong to a group forces kids into choices that are not easy. Cliques, groups, or gangs act as havens from the dominant adult world of supervision and restrictions. The commonality that bonds youngsters together can be wholesome and productive by providing support, a measure of independence, and harmless fun. That same commonality can persuade a student to use. Just as groups focus on music, sports, computers, or chess, they also center on use and abuse. Rarely does a youngster who is not a user hang out with a using group. The conspiracy of using demands that all participate; without that common experience, there is discomfort on all sides.

For example, transferring to a new high school means meeting all new friends. Users inevitably find a using group almost immediately and receive instant acceptance into the group. It's like radar. Social acceptance is seldom that easy for a straight student. The common bond of collectively concealing their use from parents, teachers, and other authority figures unites groups of users. Each new recruit swells their ranks and reinforces their belief that using is practically universal.

Youngsters choose their fashions, music, and heroes based on what is "in" or "cool." In the same way, the values of a teenage subculture are often so attractive that the family values learned at home are temporarily put aside. Approval from home becomes less important than approval by peers.

PAIN AND STRESS

Just as most adults willingly accept a shot of novocaine from dentists to block physical pain, some use tranquilizers to ease emotional pain. But adults do not have a monopoly on emotional pain.

When childhood gives way to adolescence, many youngsters have entered the most stressful, anxiety-laden years of their lives. The process of growing up can be almost unbearable. Most teenagers have deep doubts about their ability to make and hold friends, to find a mate, or to choose and hold a satisfying job. These worries over personal inadequacy sometimes trigger destructive choices, including drugs, alcohol, and even suicide.

Stress builds pressure, which in turn demands relief. Coping with stress is a fundamental part of adolescence because children in their teens begin facing problems that their parents can no longer fix. When playmates call children names in the sandbox, Mom's love can usually make the pain go away. When a teenager isn't invited to the big party, though, Mom probably won't know about it; even if she did, she probably couldn't perform the same miracle. The independence that teenagers are moving toward also moves them further away from the nurturing of their parents, the very source of most of their reassurance and support. If they fill this gap by learning to cope with the vicissitudes of life by turning to uppers and downers, they will never develop the resilience and toughness life demands. Invariably adolescents in treatment centers have poor coping skills.

GLOBAL ISSUES

Sometimes teenagers who turn to abuse carry a hopelessness of spirit because they perceive the world as a dismal place. They cite the threat of nuclear war, the hypocrisy of society, or a depressing economic future. When like-minded kids cluster together, they can reinforce each other's doomsday attitude. This perception creates a dark cloud over their lives compared to other youngsters who are aware of the same factors but hold a far more optimistic outlook.

The root of this gloom lies less with the state of the world than with the youngsters themselves. Concern over the state of today's world simply doesn't justify irresponsible behavior. Logic may not carry much weight with these teenagers, but the facts are that the world has recorded almost fifty years of history since the dropping of the first atomic bomb, the hypocrisy quotient in society hasn't changed in decades, and the only certain thing about the economy is that it will change.

Any teenager who genuinely feels defeated by the state of today's world should receive some counseling. Those who try to use this pessimistic outlook as an excuse for dropping out, giving up, and blotting out the world through chemicals are either irresponsible, lazy, or both.

CULTURAL PERSUASION

Our culture encourages children to believe that there are products that can lighten almost all their problems. Most of these products are similar to alcohol and drugs in that they promise instant gratification. Can't sleep? Take a pill. Too fat? Drink liquid protein. Lost a game? Have a beer. Win a game? Have a beer. (The breweries can't lose on this one.) Celebrating an anniversary? Buy a bottle of wine. Under stress? Take a stress vitamin.

These products play into the user mentality, which is to find swift external relief (instant gratification). Products require nothing except the money to pay for them: no introspection, no sacrifice, no changing your way of life. The message is that for a few bucks you can make your life a lot better, almost instantly, with no sweat on your part. None of these products are illegal but they embrace the same underlying approach: solutions through an external substance. They sound too good to be true; often that is exactly the case.

HISTORICAL PRECEDENT

The abuse of alcohol and drugs is not new to our time. Three thousand years ago, Homer wrote about Greek sailors whose chewing of lotus leaves so entranced them that they wanted to abandon their journey home and stay with the lotus-eaters forever. Almost every culture throughout history has found a way to alter moods. Some cultures sought a higher human state by extending the boundaries of the mind; some tried to increase sensual awareness; and some simply wanted to forget their troubles.

Normally the leaves, fruit, or roots of plants were the catalysts for these experiences. But in areas where the right plants weren't available, people developed physical techniques such as fasting, meditating, whirling or spinning rapidly, and other methods to provide the same euphoric rush of feelings. Within the fitness movement there is much talk about a "runner's high," today's version of seeking a natural euphoria. The continuous quest for these experiences through the ages is proof that there exists at least some kind of universal curiosity about mood-altering substances—if not a basic human drive.

The historical thread of use and abuse through eras and cultures may make a fascinating story, but what concerns us is the chapter that our own culture is writing today. Today's major choices for mood altering are alcohol, street drugs, and prescription drugs; unfortunately teenagers find it almost as easy to participate as adults do.

Chapter Three

Protection and Prevention

When we made our homes childproof for our toddlers, we rearranged physical objects such as matches, knives, and medicines. We also used barriers such as playpens and folding gates to block stairways. As kids grow, protection becomes more complex and difficult. They stray farther from home, and forces that parents can't control exert strong influence. When parents ask "Where in the world did my kid get that stuff?" they are really asking, "How did this happen in our family?"

Today both alcohol and illegal drugs are readily available to teenagers who want them. They can pilfer alcohol from home supplies, buy it from obliging older friends, or obtain it from stores that are careless about checking identification cards. Illegal drugs seem to be available wherever teenagers go—in schools, in the parks, at bowling alleys, and in shopping centers. Alcohol and drugs are almost as easy for teenagers to get as cigarettes or soft drinks. And that fact is unlikely to change. It's up to parents to teach the right attitudes and support them.

A juvenile police officer once astonished a high school faculty by predicting that he could go to a small shopping center two blocks from the school and buy drugs. He was back in twenty minutes with a bag of grass. He had made his point about the easy availability of illegal drugs.

The best protection system may be a good parent: wise, understanding, loving, patient, firm, and with a large measure of empathy. Sometimes even that isn't enough. An important part of being a responsible parent requires taking action and holding positions that will reduce the chances of your children slipping into usage without someone noticing. The following suggestions all work best when parents establish them early, but there isn't a better time to start than today. Begin by clearly saying NO!

EMPHASIZING YOUR POSITION

Your position on drugs and alcohol must be NO and you must never waver from it. Despite your personal habits or beliefs, there are two compelling arguments that make it imperative:

1. It is against the law.

2. It is an unnecessary, dangerous risk for youngsters.

In case you ever feel tempted to ease off on your position, list all the people you know who have improved their lives by using alcohol and drugs. It's a nonexistent list. Then list all the people you know whose lives have been damaged. We don't let infants play with matches, and we don't let children experiment with drugs and alcohol.

We don't let them experiment with vandalism, burglary, or arson, either.

In surveys, kids who DO NOT USE inevitably name their parents as the most influential factor in their decision.

TEACHING RESPONSIBLE USE DOESN'T WORK

At one time, many people held the belief that children should be taught to drink at the proper occasions and in the proper amounts. They often used the example of Italy, a country where table wine is as much a part of family mealtimes as a fork and spoon. Italians seem to have a low incidence of alcoholism, and drunkenness is rare. The popular theory was that the constant access to alcohol caused children to accept wine as a drink, as in "food and drink," rather than considering it a forbidden stimulant. They also learned to drink in a controlled atmosphere— under the watchful eyes of parents.

Like some wines, the custom does not travel well. The *National Institute on Alcohol Abuse* abandoned the idea of teaching responsible use because it was counterproductive. It didn't work because the compulsive drinker can't control his consumption any more than most people can stop with one peanut. Trying to convince abusing-type people that they can learn to drink responsibly is irresponsible.

*The answer is not to teach children how to drink but to teach them **not** to drink.*

THE ART OF SAYING NO

Your kids are going to face constant opportunities to become involved with using. The opportunities are everywhere, and it is impossible for parents to be a shield to all the temptations. Those who study decision-making seem to agree that some adults have trouble being decisive because they never learned to make decisions when they were children. They didn't get enough practice at small choices like which sweater to wear, which cereal to eat, or which friend to invite to a birthday party. When more important decisions arose, they were unsure of themselves and looked to others for guidance.

If no one has prepared your kids by teaching them how to refuse, they may participate by default, not knowing how to say NO. Make sure that your kids can be decisive on decisive issues by preparing them in advance. One way is to discuss with them situations that they probably will encounter, such as:

- insistence by a host at a party to participate by having a beer like everyone else;

- an offer by friends to try smoking grass because it feels so great;

- an invitation to a party where some "really good stuff" will be passed around;

- a request by a close friend to "get blasted" with her because her parents are talking divorce.

Saying NO to temptation is never easy, and it helps some youngsters to rehearse answers that they can use when under pressure from peers. They are certain to hear these kinds of statements: "It's fun" "Everybody does it" "Don't be chicken" "Nobody's going to know" and other tempting phrases and challenges. Encourage your children to tell you where and how the offers are likely to be made and how they plan to respond. It's important for your kids to find the kind of responses that will be accepted as NO by their peers but also will allow them to save face.

If possible, play the devil's advocate with your children, letting them respond to your most persuasive arguments. There's nothing like a dress rehearsal to get ready for the real thing. We have to teach our little children to say NO to strangers, and we also have to teach our adolescents to say NO to their friends.

> *The best response may be the simplest: "No, thank you."*

A REFUSAL TECHNIQUE

In some parts of the country, schools are teaching students refusal techniques that help them avoid messy situations. One such technique involves three steps. Explain it to your children as follows:

1. *Ask Questions.* When someone, especially someone who is not a close friend, asks you to go somewhere or do something that is unfamiliar, ask questions before you agree. Questions such as "Where is It?"

"Will adults be present?" "Who will be there?" "Will
there be drinking?" "Will there be drugs available?"

It's important to find out exactly what will happen
before you agree to anything.

2. *Explain Your Refusal.* You may choose not to go for
many reasons: you are afraid to be where others are
using drugs or alcohol - you've made a promise to
your parents - you don't want to get involved in
anything that is illegal - it might make you ineligible
- you simply don't want to begin using - you don't
enjoy that sort of fun.

3. *Offer An Alternative.* After refusing, make a counter
offer by issuing an invitation to a different activity
like a movie, a game, roller-skating, or coming over
to your house. This shows that you appreciate the
offer and you are willing to be friends. Make sure
the person understands that you are rejecting the
activity and not the friendship.

PLEDGES AND PROMISES

Some of us remember the temperance (abstinence)
pledges that we signed as youngsters in our churches. It
was an attempt to get an early commitment in the hope
that we would honor that pledge lifelong. Some movements, like "Say NO to Drugs," are reviving this tactic.
Also, some schools are encouraging student leaders, such
as outstanding athletes, to publicly pledge to keep their
lives clean. The idea is to make it popular to say NO—an
idea that deserves widespread support. It is peer pressure

of the very best kind because it counters a primary claim of the user: "Everybody does it."

When a student makes a public commitment to say NO, it does more than act as a model for other kids. That student also gains personally because making the pledge publicly provides one more reason for staying clean—after all, a promise is a promise. This alone can reduce overtures made to a nonuser by those who use.

If there is a program of this kind in your area, support it personally and encourage your kids to join it. Provided the parent does not use coercion to obtain it, a personal promise from child to parent may be appropriate. When given in the right spirit, it is a wonderful gift of peace of mind for a child to give a parent.

A SAFE RIDE HOME

There are organizations that promote a safe ride home for teenagers who are in no condition to drive. One version is for parents and children to make an agreement that obligates parents to provide a ride home, no questions asked, when children so request. Aimed at stopping accidents on the roadway, an agreement like this can bring peace of mind to parents.

Critics contend that the idea promotes an irresponsible attitude—"I can get drunk because my parents will come and get me"—which implicitly seems to give permission. Advocates maintain that since youngsters will make mistakes, it makes sense to lessen the damages. Part of the agreement often is that there will be no hassle at the scene but that the problem will not be overlooked, only delayed until the following day.

Any parent would exchange the inconvenience of providing a ride home for the prevention of another teenage accident by an incapacitated driver. In addition, the safe ride home may be your first indication that your child is drinking and sets the stage for both of you to face the situation. Just be certain that if you make such an agreement, your child understands that a safe ride home doesn't mean that all is forgotten or forgiven; it simply means a brief postponement.

PARENTS' NETWORK

In some parts of the country parents organize into networks. Members pledge that youngsters will not be allowed drugs or liquor in their homes and that the parents will personally supervise parties from start to finish. Some networks are very elaborate, publishing newsletters and member lists, and others are informal, word-of-mouth groups.

Networks not only provide a way to exchange information but also provide mutual support from parent to parent. It helps to know which other parents are holding the line just like you are. If there isn't a parents' network in your area, try to get schools or churches to help you organize one. They don't happen automatically, and in some communities the climate simply isn't ripe.

After an incident where her underage son had come home from an afternoon graduation open-house smelling of liquor, Jeff's mother was angry. A phone call to the host parents got nowhere; the hosts would accept no responsibility for serving liquor to minors and felt that what they did in their own home was nobody's business. After hitting that dead end, she decided to form a parents' network. She found very little enthusiasm, a tad of resentment, and mostly apathy. She gave up.

The following year a seventeen-year-old boy's parents found him dead in his car in the driveway at 6:00 A.M. Because he was too drunk to drive the night before, friends had driven him home; they thought he would wake up in an hour or so and go into the house. He never woke up. He had overdosed on alcohol. The incident stunned the community, but no one took action.

Now, three years later, the students in the high school are organizing a campaign on their own. So far there is no evidence that the parents will mobilize with them. Perhaps a little child shall lead them; perhaps not.

KNOW THEIR FRIENDS

Make certain that all kids feel welcome at your house. When they are there, you are not only providing a wholesome place to meet, but also you are learning things. Peers have tremendous influence on teenagers. Nine out of ten kids say that they took their first puff on a joint or their first sip of beer in the presence of their friends, as a way to impress them. Seeing and listening to their friends gives you at least a rough assessment of the influence they are likely to have. Make it clear that you want to know their friends—especially new ones—so that they can become family friends as well.

If you don't think that friends are important, consider this: almost 100 percent of the time a user's best friend is someone who is also a user. Also, when kids are in trouble, they choose their friends as the number one source of help. Parents rank number two.

WHERE ARE THEY?

Require that your children always tell you where they are going and when they will be back. You have a right to be free of constant worry. You also deserve a phone call if plans change and the time of arrival will be different. This reporting system should be established early so that it becomes a family ritual. Imposing it on a high school senior will seem very restrictive, but that doesn't mean it shouldn't be done.

It helps if you play by the same rules and extend the same courtesy to the children by always informing them of your whereabouts.

IDLE HANDS

"Idle hands are the devil's playground" is not only an adage but also almost a prophesy. Busy youngsters, too, can get into trouble, but it is a fact that serious abuse requires time—time to plan a meeting place, time to arrange for the substances and share the costs, time to invite and include others, and a block of time when it is safe to be bombed without risk of discovery.

Boredom and loneliness are virtual invitations to try something new, to take a few chances, and to accept overtures from new friends. When kids consume time in wholesome activities with few dead spots, it's more difficult to get involved in heavy abuse. That's why one goal of aftercare treatment is to get kids involved in satisfying activities that gobble up their free time so they aren't milling around looking for something to do. Make sure your kids have an assortment of worthwhile things to choose among; don't let them go looking for trouble.

KEY PEOPLE

Work at getting to know any other adults who are key people in the life of your youngster. They may be teachers, coaches, church workers, playground supervisors, or friendly neighbors. These are the people who can act as a baseline for the behavior of your youngster. You can check with them when you sense that things may be going wrong, and you need a second opinion from another perspective. It is also true that when people know you personally, they are more likely to come to you if they have concerns about your children.

PARTY TIME

If you believe surveys, you can be certain that alcohol or drugs are available at many teenage parties. Beer busts and keggers are drifting downward to younger and younger party-goers.

If you throw a party at your house for kids, you are irresponsible if you allow any alcohol or drugs, and you are naive if you believe every guest will honor your request for a straight party. Surveillance at a teenage party is no easy trick, but it is your responsibility.

When your kids attend parties elsewhere, call in advance to thank the family for entertaining your kids. You should also find out if the parents will be home, and when the party begins and ends. Ask if alcohol will be served, and make your position clear. You must not let another parent change the standards that you set for your children. Some parents think limited drinking under supervision is okay; it isn't when they are minors. Although the parent network mentioned earlier makes these calls easier, make the call even if you have to do it solo. If you find an occasional parent who gives you grief, it's a good sign your community could use a network.

A party at a home where the parents are out of town is an accident waiting to happen. News of an unsupervised party travels fast; even if the original plan was innocent, party crashers can change the complexion of activities in minutes. Never, never allow your children to throw a party in your home unless you are present; never knowingly let them attend a house party without verified adult supervision present.

A sixteen-year-old sophomore girl told an incredulous teacher this story about a Saturday-night party. Unfortunately it was true. It seems at a house party for sophomores and juniors there was so much drinking that a half-dozen kids passed out cold. In addition, two junior boys gave a demonstration on how to sniff cocaine and offered to initiate others. Three kids gave it a try. When asked where the parents were, the girl replied, "They stayed upstairs through the whole party except when the father stuck his head in and said that the local liquor store closed in an hour; if anyone needed liquor, he would get it for them."

How would you like to have your youngster attend that party?

Incidentally, if you as a parent are responsible for serving or supplying alcohol to minors, you are unquestionably breaking the law. Some naive parents gave teenage parties where kids have gotten drunk and died in auto accidents on the way home. How would you like to live with that? How would you like to live with the possible legal liability?

STAYING OUT OVERNIGHT

Users are always looking for ways to conceal their use from their parents. One common trick is to stay over at a friend's house or, even better, to say that they are. Once they have covered the home front, they can safely get bombed, sleep it off, and then return home in the morning. The best bet is to stay in a home where the parents are away or at least where there is irresponsible supervision. Kids also may pitch in for a motel room and then are free to party all night.

Another version is to call home late and plead car trouble or some other excuse for sleeping over rather than returning home at such a late hour. If situations like this come up, insist that you talk to the host parents and make sure that it's legitimate. If your kids are reluctant to put the parents on the line and instead agree to come home, note how long it takes before they get home. They may be delaying to allow time to sober up. If staying out overnight happens with any frequency, you should get very nervous.

SAYING GOOD NIGHT

Teenagers grow up, parents age, and the bedtime gap closes until the kids are up long after parents turn in for the night. Setting hours is the parent's prerogative and the only reasonable way to prevent worrisome nights waiting for the front door to open. It helps if the hours match up with the norms in the community. Hardly anyone knows of kids who have gotten into trouble because they had to come home on time. As most of us remember, not many good things happen after the movies are over and the restaurants close.

One mother established a wonderful ritual that is recommended highly. If she was in bed when the youngsters came home, her children knocked on her bedroom door and then came in and kissed their mother good night. This practice accomplished a lot besides giving mom restful nights. She always knew exactly when they came home and what kind of shape they were in. The kids always knew that there was that final, brief inspection. Simple but diabolical.

PRIVACY VERSUS SECRECY

One of the hardest lines to walk is to show interest in your children without prying into their affairs. There may come a time when you have to disregard privacy to unravel a mystery by searching personal belongings. Kids have a right to their secrets but not if they are harmful and illegal. Home is not a court of law with rules of evidence and built-in protection. Your personal code will determine how and if you decide to make a search, but uncovering physical proof of use wipes away all doubts and brings the problem into daylight.

One mother knew that her son was smoking pot in his basement bedroom, but he denied it. She couldn't catch him even after searching his room several times. Finally she mentioned it to an older brother who was no longer living at home but had stopped by. He immediately went to the basement, lifted up a ceiling tile and found a stash of marijuana and a pipe. The older brother confessed that he had used the same hiding place for his X-rated magazines.

When both his mother and his brother confronted the youngster with the evidence, he gave up pot, mostly because of his brother's street smarts, which made him difficult to fool.

PARENTAL EXPECTATIONS

Family values and expectations are the natural burden of every child. It's impossible for children not to measure themselves against what they think their parents expect.

When they feel that they are not measuring up, they become vulnerable to sinking self-esteem, feelings of failure, and depression; states of mind that make mood-changing substances attractive.

We all have seen the ridiculous living stereotypes of stagedoor mothers and jockstrap-mentality fathers who live vicariously through their children's achievements. But subtler expectations can be equally harmful.

For example, parents almost invariably overestimate the scholastic ability of their children. They pay little attention to standardized test scores or actual scholastic performance, insisting that "The brains are there but he doesn't use them." Every time unrealistic expectations are present, whether it's school grades, athletic ability, popularity, or any level of talent, they set the stage for a child to feel inadequate. High-powered, successful parents usually expect their children to emulate them, as if achievement were automatically passed on through the genes.

Please take the time to analyze your expectations. If you can, explain them to your child, not as requirements, but as projections of what you would like your child to become. You might be wiser and serve your child better to emphasize expectations like being courteous, thoughtful, kind, honest, and giving one's best effort. Those are within every child's reach. Unrealistic expectations simply add unnecessary pressure at a time when no youngster needs it.

Expect each of your children to be different; you didn't reproduce clones. Too many youngsters in treatment centers lament that they knew that they could never hope to match their siblings. Therefore, they believed that they could never satisfy their parents.

LOVE THY CHILDREN

The question for most of us as parents is not whether we love our children; of course we do. The question is: Do they know that we love them? There is an old Scandinavian joke about the husband who was standing at the burial of his wife when a friend sympathetically said, "She was a wonderful woman; I'm sure you're going to miss her." Lars replied, "Yah, you bet. We were married over fifty years, and I loved her so much that once I almost told her."

It's presumptuous to try to tell anyone how to show love to their children. Some of us are demonstrative and some of us aren't. Some can hug and kiss; some can give praise easily; and some can communicate their feelings freely; others can't. Each of us has to be true to our own personality.

But it is a fact that kids in chemical dependency treatment programs frequently feel unloved. The emotions that arise in a family when a child is in crisis often surprise the children. They are just as astonished by the outpouring of love and concern as the parents are to learn that their child felt unloved. This might be a good time to take an inventory of your love index. If you decide that your feelings are much stronger than your actions, invest some thought and energy into making your youngster feel loved.

To borrow from Shakespeare, "The quality of parental love (nee mercy) is not strained, it droppeth as the gentle rain from heaven upon the place beneath. It is twice blessed; it blesseth him that gives and him that takes." Why not go for a double blessing?

SETTING THE LIMITS

Although teenagers seldom see it that way, insisting on rules and restrictions also can be a form of love. Parents who care will take some precautionary steps that may be unpopular but pay off in the long run. Being discontent with some of those restrictions is part of the price of being listed as a dependent on the family tax return.

Mark felt disappointed by his parents' insistence on a midnight curfew that was absolutely nonnegotiable. He claimed that he was the only senior at school with such restrictive hours and constantly complained that his mother had yet to enter the 20th century. Finally, when his mother had heard enough, she told him this: "Everybody has a cross to bear. Allison has a retarded sister, Jimmy's mother died when he was seven, Jack has a father who throws wrenches at him, Brenda is a diabetic, and your cross is having Attila the Hun as a mother—count your blessings."

Mark continued to complain but without enthusiasm.

RATING YOUR KID

Parents are busy people and tend to assume all is well with their children, mostly expecting them to measure up to family standards. Sometimes measuring up is not as easy as it looks but parents often take it for granted.

Before falling asleep one night Betsy's parents were talking about how pleased they were with the way their daughter was growing up. They thought of a special way to show her: an unofficial report card signed by both of them. It looked like this:

Anthropology (studying adolescent boys)   **A**
Biology (number of living protoplasms growing
        in bedroom)   **C**
Composition (writing letters to grandmother)   **A**
Criminology (not being one)   **A**
Foreign Language (used while talking on the telephone
        to friends)   **A**
Health (nutrition and personal habits)   **A**
Home Economics (making popcorn)   **A**
Math (staying within allowance)   **A**
Music (singing while working around the house)   **A**
Psychology (handling pesky younger brother)   **A**

Letting kids know that you are aware of the plusses in their lives and of the problems they DON'T cause you is part of being a good parent. Find a way to do that now and then.

SWALLOWING THE IMPLAUSIBLE

The trust between parent and child is as delicate as a butterfly and just as beautiful. Parents cherish and cling to that trust and can put common sense on the back burner. But when things aren't adding up, stories don't jibe, and your instincts are disturbing your subconscious, take some action! If nothing else, try the story on another adult and get an objective opinion. Don't be blinded by the brilliance of your own genes. No parent ever helped a youngster by believing lies. Users learn to be world-class liars.

SHAKING THE FAMILY TREE

There is growing scientific evidence for a theory that matches up with what experienced chemical dependency workers have observed often—abuse seems to run in families. Our purpose is not to rehash the nature versus nurture argument (whether children are predisposed to abuse or if they simply imitate the behavior of other family members) but to put you on the alert to what may be an important finding. We may eventually discover that, in our genes, some of us carry and pass on to our children a susceptibility to abuse.

If we acknowledge the possibility that some of us can transmit a genetic trigger for abuse, then we have an obligation to alert our children to the fact that they are in a high-risk group. To play it safe, take a close look at both sides of the family for a few generations back. If there are abusers in the family tree, make certain that your children know that they may be in a high-risk category. If there are adopted or foster children in your household, the search may not be easy, but you may want to pursue it; it's for their sake, not yours.

LOOKING IN THE MIRROR

Children of one alcoholic parent have a higher incidence of alcoholism—four times higher—than children of nonalcoholic parents. When both parents are alcoholics, the odds soar even higher. Research shows that there is a significant correlation between parental use/abuse patterns and those that the children eventually choose for themselves. In other words, your kids probably will follow your example.

If you abuse alcohol or drugs, your behavior makes a much stronger statement than any advice you may try to give. The only safe course for parents is to clean up their act first. At the very least this means controlled, responsible use of legal substances only. You cannot ignore your responsibility as the most powerful role model in the life of your child.

WHEN PARENTS DRINK

It's not very realistic to expect every parent to give up alcohol and become a model of abstinence for their children. Wonderful, but not realistic. Drinking yourself while forbidding your children to drink is not as hypocritical as it appears. The factors that make the rules different for you compared to your children are age and maturity.

You can buy, drink, and serve alcohol with immunity from the law. A minor cannot. In all states there is a legal age for drinking just as there is a legal age for obtaining a driver's license. If you do either before your time, you are asking for trouble with the law.

Secondly, as stated elsewhere, adolescence is a time of growth and development, and we know that alcohol can limit that normal maturation process. It simply isn't worth the risk of long-term damage. (See Dave's Case, Chapter One.) Adults have passed through that period and are no longer so vulnerable.

You may want to consider a frank discussion with your children about your personal drinking habits—how you began and why you continue. Expressing your true motivations may be enlightening for everyone. You may get some tough questions, criticism, and some requests to change your habits; so be prepared to handle them or don't bring up the subject.

Of course disapproval can be carried to extremes. An example would be old Mrs. Gunderson who chastised her pastor after his sermon on moderation in all things, including alcohol. In his defense he reminded her that the Bible was full of references to the drinking of wine and that even Jesus drank wine on several occasions recorded in the Bible. After a pause she replied, "You know, I never liked that about Him."

A WRITTEN RECORD

Parents who are diary keepers by nature have a distinct advantage over the rest of us because they are in the habit of recording events. Commonly, parents of students in treatment are astonished at the number of different negative incidents that had to happen before the parents realized that something was haywire. Negative memories fade quickly; those that remain often appear to be separate incidents rather than parts of a pattern.

If you record each incident that makes you uneasy, you have an excellent chance of connecting the dots and seeing a clear picture. The warning signs in the next chapter will help you decide what might be significant.

CHECKING IT OUT

Most parents who have had experience with abuse will tell you that their biggest mistake was keeping everything to themselves. We tend to pretend things are okay when they aren't, rather than admit that our kids might be heading down the wrong road.

When in doubt, spit it out! Find someone who will listen and give you an objective opinion. A professional counselor at school or in a community agency can provide an invaluable perspective. Don't let family pride block the chance to get some relief or some advice.

PARENTS' SCOREBOARD

1. Have you made the family position clear?
2. Have you discussed how to say NO?
3. Has your youngster pledged, publicly or privately to you, not to use as a minor?
4. Do you always know where your kids are and where they hang out?
5. Do you check out all parties?
6. Are you always awake to check in your kids at bedtime?
7. Would you be pleased if your child followed the same pattern of use that you do?
8. Do you belong to a parents' network?
9. Do you know the key adults in your child's life?
10. Do you know your kid's friends by name and face?
11. Have you ever verified a fishy story?
12. Do you record confusing or suspicious incidents?

SCORING: Give yourself 3 points for a yes on questions 1 - 7; all other yes answers are worth 2 points.

CURVE: 24 - 31   World class
       18 - 23   Olympic hopeful
       12 - 17   Showing promise but needs work
       11 - 0   Better start getting in shape

Chapter Four

Warning Signs

Despite extensive research, nobody has developed any kind of indicator that can predict in advance which children are most susceptible to abuse. Every parent must be alert for warning signs which run on a scale from subtle to blatant.

SECONDARY SIGNS are those actions or behavior that abuse may be causing. An example would be withdrawing from the family and preferring solitude. The actual cause could be losing a friend, falling in love, a burst of concern about the future, OR it could be abuse.

PRIMARY SIGNS are more than warnings; they are proof. An example would be coming home drunk.

In Chapter One, Dave's parents were seeing only secondary signs in the life of a very careful user. It was a difficult case to read because abuse is not the sole cause of all secondary signs. They must be interpreted in light of your child's experiences and personality. As a rule of thumb, the more abrupt, drastic, and extensive the changes are, the higher the odds that they involve abuse.

The secondary signs that follow are not all-inclusive but are only examples of behavior changes often associated with youngsters who use. If the signs you see alarm you, it's a good idea to consult somebody else. As best you can, list the changes in writing, using the summary at the end of this chapter as a guide. Bring them to someone whose judgment you trust and ask for an objective opinion. If the person is knowledgeable about abuse it will help, because he or she will ask questions that will help clarify the situation. Your biggest mistake would be to overlook the signs and hope that they will blow over. Nobody knows more about your kid than you do, but parents can be blind; don't be bashful about asking for help in interpreting the signs that you see. School counselors, clergy members, or others accustomed to working with youth have seen hundreds of troubled youngsters and often spot tell-tale signs that parents miss.

SCHOOL PERFORMANCE

A change in performance level sometimes happens because kids are spending time and energy on acquiring and using drugs or alcohol; homework, assignment deadlines, and grades become less important. In addition, if students go through the school day partially zapped or hungover from the night before, learning conditions are not ideal. Spotting a using student in a classroom of thirty or more isn't easy for a teacher; it's possible for a student to spend the day in a fog without anyone noticing. Falling grades, reports from teachers of listlessness, sleeping during class, and unfinished assignments are serious in themselves but also are common signs of abuse. They are especially telling when the student promises improvement that never seems to materialize.

FRIENDS

All friendships are not lifelong; it isn't unusual for kids to add and drop friends as interests change. When friendships change the key is the basis for making the change. Kids can't always explain friendships and they shouldn't have to; but how they spend their time with friends is important. If you're not sure where they go and what they do, and the new friends are never brought home for introductions, get out your worry beads.

If your child spends much time away from home at a particular house, it may be a warm, welcoming, wholesome place or it may be a sign of a free-wheeling household, which allows behavior that you would not tolerate in your home. The safe course is to check.

Be especially alert if your child suddenly drops all the old friends and replaces them with a new crowd. Users and nonusers don't mix very well; running with a using crowd is a dead giveaway.

HANGOUTS

Hangouts often change when friends change. When your youngster leaves the house without saying where he's going or with whom, and then returns with vague answers such as "We drove around" or "We hung out at the shopping center" or "We went to a kid's house," you should prick up your ears.

TELECOMMUNICATIONS

Some teenagers seem to have a telephone growing out of their ear—a normal condition at that age. But your alarm should go off if phone traffic picks up late in the evening, especially if conversations are very short. Short calls can mean that the teenager is making last-minute plans for drug traffic. If your kid never takes these calls in your presence but insists on privacy, it's a double warning. The same thing applies if kids drop by the house but stay in the car. Short curbside visits are often the preferred delivery method.

MONEY TALKS

The second biggest shock parents get when kids reveal their using history is how much hard-earned money they have wasted. The biggest shock is always how long and how often their kids had been using undetected.

Cash flow can be a tip-off to abuse. If your kids have allowances or part-time jobs, try to monitor how they spend their money without acting like the I.R.S. Watch savings accounts as well because an abuser can clean them out in a hurry.

Desperation has led many youngsters to steal from their parents. If money is missing and you can't pinpoint the leakage, start playing detective; if you feel seriously alarmed, bait a trap. Theft from family members is often a sign of a youngster who is losing the battle against abuse.

If unexplained cash shows up in your youngster's hands, you'd better ask for an accounting and then follow up. The classic way to support a growing habit is to become a small-time dealer.

JACK'S TRUNK

This is a true story describing what happened when an alert school counselor called a tenacious father about money matters.

Counselor. I'm calling with some information that I'm uneasy about. I didn't know whether to call or not but I think if Jack were my son, I'd want to know. Three times in the last few weeks staff members have seen Jack by his locker with large sums of money, not $10 or $20 but more like $100. He is exchanging it with other students. I plan to see Jack and ask him about it and I also will ask him not to bring so much money to school. Kids don't need that kind of money at school, and we always worry about thefts.

Father. This sounds funny. Jack's allowance is $10 a week and he has to buy his school lunch out of that, so I can't understand where the money is coming from. Thanks for calling, and I'll check into it on my end.

. . . few days later:

Father. This is Jack's father calling you back. I've solved the mystery. Apparently Jack and his buddies have started playing some pretty heavy poker and Jack has been the big winner. Anyway, I told him that he's a little too young for serious gambling, and the poker games are over. I also told him not ever to carry extra money to school. But thanks a lot for calling.

Counselor. That's OK but I'm still uneasy. I know who Jack's buddies are and the kids I've seen around his locker are both boys and girls and not necessarily his best friends. Jack's a good kid and a solid citizen but I can't help feeling that something is going on here. I asked him myself why he was carrying so much money and he told me that it was a birthday present from his grandmother.

Father. Why would he say that? His birthday is in the summer. I believe Jack about the poker game. Have you seen him with any big money lately?

Counselor. No, but his gym teacher told me that he saw Jack and two other kids exchanging money in the locker room. Jack said he was collecting the last payment on a car stereo he had sold the other boy.

Father. Jack does have a car stereo but I didn't think he had sold it. This doesn't sound like him. I don't know what to say.

Counselor. I hope I'm wrong but I'm worried about two possibilities—that he might be taking bets, acting as a bookie, or that he might be selling something illegal.

Father. You mean like drugs?

Counselor. Maybe.

Father. Can't be. There must be an explanation for this. I'll talk to Jack again and get to the bottom of this. Don't worry, if anything shady is going on it's going to stop right now. I know Jack and I can't believe he'd do anything so stupid, he's too smart for that. But I'll check, you can count on it.

Follow-up

The father's uneasiness won out over his confidence in Jack and he went home from work and looked through Jack's room but found nothing suspicious. In Jack's car, however, an old junker his parents allowed him to drive evenings and weekends, his father found a notebook in the glove compartment with a series of names and numbers, clearly a record book of some kind. In the trunk in a cardboard box, underneath some tennis balls, a baseball glove, and an old sweatshirt, were several boxes of plastic bags and over $1400 in cash.

When his father confronted Jack and put the pressure on, the story came out. Jack had smoked pot a few times, and then another boy at school had persuaded him to become a small-time dealer. Jack got a percentage of his sales and rationalized it by saving the money for college; he knew college would be a financial burden for his parents. Fortunately Jack himself was a very light user, and not hung up on drugs. He was willing to give up the easy money and occasional use to repair the rupture he had caused in the trust and respect his parents had had in him.

The only option the family gave Jack was which charity would get the $1400. He chose the *United Way*.

By accepting the possibility that his son might not be perfect, Jack's father stopped a very nasty beginning before serious trouble came up.

PHYSICAL SYMPTOMS

Sometimes physical symptoms are not so obvious. Many kids have fooled their parents, operating on a slight buzz (semi-intoxicated or semi-high) most of their waking hours. Generally speaking, breath with an odd smell (or heavily disguised by chewing gum or mints), unfocused or unclear eyes, and speech that is slow, slurred, or inappropriate deserves investigation. If any of these signs appear regularly without a medical explanation, you must consider abuse as a possibility.

Extensive abuse of alcohol or drugs can cause serious physical disorders but they take time to develop. If your youngster has a persistent cough, runny nose, sore throat, upset stomach, or experiences a steady weight loss, check with a doctor. If the symptoms don't respond to treatment, ask the doctor if abuse could be the cause.

PERSONALITY CHANGES

Nothing is more frustrating to a parent than a child who is not himself. All of us have said things such as "Snap out of it" or "What in the world is wrong with you?" when uncharacteristic behavior puzzles us. Unpredictability, impulsiveness, exaggerated responses to small frustrations, rapid changes of mood, and especially reduced energy, drive, and motivation can frustrate parents. Not only that, but they also can be indicators of chemicals that are acting as change agents within the bodily system.

LONG-LASTING DEPRESSION

Teenagers are notorious for overreacting. They go from the top of the world to the dumpster in the time it takes to bat an eye, especially if the wrong eye is batted. But they are also resilient and bounce back almost as fast. When a youngster gets stuck in a trough of depression, it can be the sign of someone who is ripe for mood-altering substances or the sign of one who is already on the way to heavy using.

Youth is the time for fun, at least for the most part. When your kid isn't having any, and can't be shaken out of depression, it may be time to opt for some counseling. When sadness, self-depreciation, negative expressions, listlessness, hopelessness, and low self-esteem hang on and on, seek professional help.

A TENDER MOMENT

After school Jon came into the kitchen, sitting dejectedly while his mother prepared supper. He had seemed sad and subdued for some time, which had worried his mother. Jon was well aware of the expectations his parents had for him, especially academically, and the reminders usually came in the form of disapproval followed by pep talks. This night his mother took a different tack.

Mother. Jon, you look as though you've lost your best friend, things must be going pretty bad.

Jon. You're not kidding.

Mother. School?

Jon. School and everything.

Mother. Are you failing?

Jon. Yes.

Mother. Everything?

Jon. Just about everything.

Mother. That doesn't mean that Jon himself is a failure; it only means that you aren't doing something right.

Jon looked up gratefully and after a few more minutes of small talk left the kitchen. After supper he came back to his mother and said, "I have to tell you something." Although she had been suspicious, his mother was astonished at the story that poured out, describing a long period of heavy drug taking. Jon had been near the bottom and his mother's words, although they may have seemed insignificant to an outsider, had opened the floodgates. The family immediately contacted a chemical dependency counselor and began the process of recovery.

His mother is sure that if she had scolded Jon that evening, as in the past, he would have stayed in his shell and continued to conceal his abuse. His mother's words had tipped the scale.

LYING AND DECEIT

Total honesty is probably beyond the pale of most human beings. It's a rare child who hasn't attempted to "con" his parents when things get a little sticky. "Who ate the last cookie?" is a question that doesn't always get a straightforward response, at least not in most homes. As parents we try to be alert for these attempts at situational ethics and reinforce the old adage that "Honesty is the best policy." It is best to settle the issue of honesty in childhood, when attempts at deceit are clumsy and transparent, and the family values can develop a healthy root system.

An entirely different kind of lying and deceit occurs when a youngster knows that his behavior is absolutely wrong by family and legal standards. This is true for alcohol and drug consumption just as surely as it is for shoplifting, burglary, or speeding.

Assuming the family position is clear on minors using, a youngster will go to elaborate lengths to conceal his use from home. As usage increases, the lies become more numerous, more complex, and more revealing if only parents can listen to them with an objective ear. When your antennae are picking up disturbing vibrations of deceit, it's time to get to the bottom of things.

CHECKLIST FOR WARNING SIGNS

1. Have old friends disappeared and been replaced by kids that you don't know?

2. Have your kid's hangouts changed recently?

3. Are there many short, late-night phone calls?

4. Do you sense that your kid is deceiving you?

5. Is school performance deteriorating?

6. Are you uneasy about the way your child is handling money?

7. Do colds, sore throats, poor appetites, or headaches seem to hang on?

8. Have you observed negative personality changes recently?

SCORING: Count 3 points for a yes on #1-4, two points for a yes on #5-8

   0-5   So far, so good

   6-10   Stay on the alert

   11-15 Investigate further

   16-20 The alarm is going off!

Chapter Five

Dealing With Suspicion

For our purposes in this book there are four categories of concern: suspicion, experimentation, use, and abuse. Suspicion takes the joy out of being a parent. It clouds our relationship with our kids because we can't decide whether to stay clear and worry, or jump in with accusations that might cause hard feelings. Remember that the secondary signs described in Chapter Four are exactly that—signs. Even in cases when all are present you can't be certain that use or abuse is the problem. Despite that uncertainty, all the signs represent changes, and most of them are undesirable; therefore it makes sense to do something to ease your anxiety and clear the air. The option explained next falls somewhere between a hands-off policy and a third-degree approach.

LOW-KEY CONFRONTATION

Take the time to think through exactly why the behavior is bothering you. Then sit down and express clearly to your child in specific terms how that behavior is affecting you as a parent. Often the effect is only increased worry and anxiety, but that alone is a legitimate reason for a discussion. Try to speak in cooperative language that makes your concern clear without being critical. Indicate that you are willing to help but are not trying to interfere. The following examples show good and bad alternatives:

Say:

"Your schoolwork is falling off and I'm worried because I've always thought that you've done your best. Now I'm afraid that you are getting discouraged about school and your grades are suffering. I'd like to help if I can."

Instead of:

"I can't understand why your grades are dropping. You're smart enough to do a lot better. Maybe you should spend more time studying and less time watching TV."

Say:

"You never talk about your old friends any more and I don't even know any of these new friends. It seems like your friends all changed at once and I'm concerned that something went wrong."

Instead of:

"I can't understand where all your old friends have gone. What did you do anyway?"

Say:

"You've been spending more and more time alone in your room with the door closed. It's okay to want privacy and you can have it. But if something has gone wrong, I'd like to know. Maybe I can't help, but at least I could quit worrying."

Instead of:

"What's the matter lately anyway? All you do is hole up in your room. Can't you find something better to do?"

Say:

"Wendy, I found out from Mrs. Carson that Jan went to the football game with the rest of the family Friday night. But you told me that you were with Jan watching TV. I know that you're not in the habit of lying to me so I've been worried that something serious has happened."

Instead of:

"Well, young lady, you'd better tell me where you were last Friday night and I want the truth this time."

As you can see, the purpose is to show loving concern and a willingness to help. Anger, criticism, and sarcasm all interfere with getting the issue out in the open. What you are after is some reassurance from your child that there is no serious problem. If there is a problem, you want to offer your support and, if appropriate, your assistance.

As if acting on your own suspicions isn't tough enough, you also must be prepared for dealing with unsettling information that may come from outsiders.

ACCEPTING BAD NEWS

We all want to believe and trust our kids, and our hackles go up very fast when outsiders make accusation that we don't like to hear. Our natural protective instincts kick in immediately. Those who work with youngsters are familiar with this "shoot the messenger" mentality and realize that some parents will impugn everyone in sight to fix the blame on anyone but the real culprit—their child.

Remember two things:

1. *Most bad news about your kids is true.* Responsible people don't like to bring bad news to parents unless it is important. It's much less trouble for them to let it go unreported.

2. *Kids in trouble often distort the truth to conceal what really happened.*

When bad news comes, it's legitimate to check the facts and verify that someone hasn't made a mistake. Once you've done that, try to be as impartial and objective as possible. The worst thing to do is assume that you must leap to the defense of your child and beat off the attackers. It is tempting to want to be a hero and get your kid off, but you're wiser to watch the wheels of justice grind before you yell foul.

Something can be learned from the story of Brad and his rah-rah father, basketball booster *par excellance*. The coach ruled Brad ineligible for the final three weeks of the basketball season because a faculty member had seen Brad drinking a beer in the school lavatory. It was a clear violation of eligibility rules, but the basketball team was trying to make the state play-off.

Brad's father was incensed. He demanded to meet with the teacher and the principal, using the meeting as a chance to insult and vilify the teacher. He also demanded that the principal dismiss the evidence and reinstate Brad. The principal refused. The next day the father was back with a lawyer and demanded that the teacher be required to take a lie detector test. The principal refused the demand and ignored the threat of a lawsuit, which was to be based on the possibility of losing college scholarship offers if Brad didn't finish the season. The father then arranged for his son to take a lie detector test. Brad failed the test. The father claimed the test was invalid. During the process of contracting with another agency to conduct a second test, his son finally admitted that the teacher was right. If Brad hadn't confessed, the father probably would have continued to press blindly forward, shouldering his son's responsibility for a foolish mistake.

TWO SIDES OF THE SAME COIN

There are so many parents of children in treatment who admit that they either ignored or down-played information from outsiders that it is worthwhile to examine how two different parents responded to almost identical incidents.

Sandy's Case

Principal. Mrs. Everson, I'm sorry to call to tell you that Sandy was found in school in possession of a pot pipe and a bag of marijuana.

Mrs. Everson. It can't be. Sandy would never use drugs; there must be a mistake.

Principal. I'm afraid it isn't a mistake. A teacher saw her loading the pipe with marijuana, and the consequences are quite serious.

Mrs. Everson. What did Sandy say? Did she have any explanation?

Principal. She claims that another girl gave her the stuff to hold but she can't identify the other girl.

Mrs. Everson. Well then, that's what happened! I don't understand why Sandy's guilty for what someone else did. Did you find the other girl?

Principal. No. But Sandy knows possession is against our rules and she must accept the penalty. Can you come to school to pick her up and meet with me so that I can explain our policy and the penalty?

Mrs. Everson. I don't understand this—why is Sandy being punished? It seems so unfair. I'm going to call my husband. Sandy is a good kid, gets good grades, and she would never use drugs. You've made a mistake and I don't like it!

Principal. I'm sorry but the penalty applies to Sandy. If you want to consult with your husband, please do, but I'll expect a call back from one of you within fifteen minutes so that we can move ahead on this.

Mrs. Everson. You bet we'll call back and you'd better find that other girl. We won't stand for this.

Follow-up

The principal enforced the policy. Sandy's parents blamed the school, bad-mouthed the principal, and believed that they had properly "backed up" their daughter. But Sandy was a steady user, and the police busted her a second time in a car full of drinking teenagers. Her parents again believed Sandy's claim that she was innocent. Within a year of the first incident Sandy was in an adolescent treatment center. She had fooled her parents right up to the end when she finally asked for help herself. These parents are classic examples of the "not-my-kid" syndrome.

Jennifer's Case

Principal. Mrs. Iverson, I'm sorry to call and tell you that a staff member found Jennifer in school in possession of marijuana and a pot pipe.

Mrs. Iverson. Are you sure that you have the right girl? Are you talking about Jennifer Iverson, a 10th grader, my daughter?

Principal. Yes, I'm afraid I am. A custodian saw her with a pipe and marijuana, and the consequences are quite serious.

Mrs. Iverson. Have you talked with Jennifer yourself? This doesn't sound possible.

Principal. Yes, I have talked with her and while she admits having the paraphernalia, she claims that another girl gave it to her to hold until after school. But she won't tell us the other girl's name.

Mrs. Iverson. Oh dear. I don't like the sound of this at all. I just can't believe that she'd do something like this. What should I do now?

Principal. I'd like you to come up to school and pick up Jennifer. I also want to talk to both of you so that I can explain the procedure we use here at school in cases like these.

Mrs. Iverson. I'm really sort of stunned. We've talked about this with her and we have never had a single suspicion of anything like this. Does this happen a lot at school? Her Dad will go crazy! Well, I'll get organized and get to school as fast as I can. I guess we'd better get to the bottom of this.

Follow-up

In the principal's office, Mrs. Iverson wouldn't accept Jennifer's story that she was holding for someone else. She put some pressure on her daughter and got the true story, which was that Jennifer had borrowed the pot and pipe and was loading it when the custodian caught her. Some friends had been urging her to try it and her plan was to try it alone in case she got sick. She didn't want anyone to know how inexperienced she was. Jennifer wound up in tears, and her mother was grateful that her experimentation had gone no further. The uproar in the family convinced Jennifer that experimentation was not worth it. Her parents reinforced that conclusion by clarifying their expectations for the future in no uncertain terms. Jennifer stayed clear of drugs and alcohol throughout the rest of her school years.

Jennifer's case illustrates an important point. It's essential to treat the first incident seriously because the earlier the discovery, the better the chances of success. With drugs and alcohol it doesn't pay to delay and hope that it will never happen again. With no reason to stop, most kids will continue.

SUMMARY

1. Don't ignore your feelings of anxiety. Initiate a discussion with your youngster by laying out disturbing signs and explaining that you feel concerned, worried, and want to help.

2. Check out fishy stories; don't be so naive as to think that your children will always be totally honest with you.

3. Don't dismiss outside information because it is unpleasant; don't run interference when your youngster has broken rules or laws. Let the responsibility fall where it belongs. That is how kids mature.

Chapter Six

The First Discovery

When you find primary evidence of use, you must confront it, analyze it, and react to it. In dealing with drugs and alcohol it isn't enough to be a good parent. It takes extra measures of patience and good sense. Some of your reactions will be perfectly normal but totally unproductive so you must be certain to do some preliminary planning before reacting.

CLEARING THE DECKS

First, don't try to confront a youngster who is not totally clear-minded and sober. Wait until the fog clears and also wait until your emotions have cooled down, even if it takes a day or two. In settings like a police station, a school office, or a public place, embarrassment often makes parents want to show their disapproval through angry outbursts. It's okay to show that emotion—your youngster probably expects it—but don't start to work on the problem until later.

Second, don't waste time and energy playing the game of "Where did we go wrong?" Parents can agonize and play and replay episodes where, if they had done something different, nothing like this would have happened. This is pure baloney. One mother, in a school office with her twin sons, each a confessed user and dealer, was naive enough to say that if she and her husband had only given them a *Camaro* instead of a *Chevy Celebrity* they wouldn't be in trouble now.

There isn't a kid over twelve in this country who doesn't know that drugs and alcohol are wrong numbers. With all the information that bombards kids in school and in the media it's inconceivable that a beginning user is uneducated.

No one forces kids to start; kids choose to start. Most begin in the company of friends, not with some stranger in a trench coat. They make the choice with their eyes wide open to the fact that not only is it illegal but also that their parents will disapprove. Put the responsibility where it belongs. This can't be stressed enough. It is so tempting to blame yourself, or friends, or the school, or the laxity of today's society, or the abundance of illegal drugs, or an indifferent police department, or whatever you can think of. Don't fall into that trap. Your kid has made a lousy choice and should be held responsible!

UNITY

A single parent doesn't have the advantage of checking signals with a spouse but must carry the burden alone. It might be a small blessing because at least a single parent needn't worry about presenting a united front. If you believe that the two of you can't work in tandem on the problem, one parent should step aside and let the other run the show. Above all, parents should never withhold negative information from one another. Kids are brilliant at playing divide and conquer and will exploit it to their advantage. Further, once you have selected a plan, stay with it; if you change, change together.

At an intake conference at a treatment center, sixteen-year-old Michelle admitted to becoming drunk many times since her parents had learned of the problem some eight months earlier. She had promised to stop, and her father believed that she had. But Michelle also revealed that her mother had caught her drunk often, but had fallen for the pleas of, "Don't tell Dad and I'll promise there will never be a next time." Obviously the father was angry and insulted, and a serious rift developed when unity was paramount. Equally important was the delay that permitted the progression to continue for another eight months.

R. A. G. E. DOESN'T WORK

There is a familiar cycle to the emotions that overpower parents when their kids get into trouble. The acronym RAGE describes that cycle:

Responsibility - as in taking it on yourself
Anger - as in expressing it
Guilt - as in wallowing in it
Embarrassment - as in feeling it

Rage is an especially appropriate word because it means violent anger. Anger never solves anything; neither do the reactions represented by RAGE. This scenario illustrates the reactions of a typical parent to the first proof of teenage drinking:

Action. Paul, seventeen, has a fender bender with the family car and is also charged with Driving While Intoxicated.

Reaction by father. "I feel like wringing his neck. How can he be so stupid, driving and drinking? We've talked about it a thousand times. I can hear my brother-in-law now: 'I hear Golden Boy had an accident.' How are we going to explain this to Gramma? And what about Mary's bridge partners; they are going to love this. Why did I ever let him have the car Friday night? I had a hunch there had been some drinking going on at those parties lately and I should have seen this coming. I also should have been smart enough to lower the deductible on the car insurance. Now I've got to call the insurance man and come up with $500 to pay our share of the damages. This accident is probably going to raise my premium, too. And I'd better do something about this drinking before it gets out of hand. Boy, if I had done this at seventeen, my Dad would have taken care of me, pronto."

As you follow these thoughts you can see the progression from anger at Paul, to embarrassment for the family image, to guilt for not being a perfect, clairvoyant parent, and finally to assuming the responsibility for cleaning up the mess. Very likely you've been through that familiar cycle in some form or another. Try to remember that those reactions may be typical, but they don't contribute to a solution.

ENCOURAGING DISCLOSURE

Once your initial, emotional reaction is over, you are ready to gather the information that you need to assess the damages. You are going to have to decide if you are dealing with experimentation or regular use. For our purposes, experimentation means one or two attempts to "try" after which the teenager makes a decision to stop. A third attempt is graduation to regular use. Obviously your best source of information is your child, and your goal is to get complete disclosure from the very beginning.

Occasionally a child blurts out the entire story at the outset. Such parents are very fortunate. More often only part of the story will be told, as kids attempt to cut their losses. The classic responses are, "This was the first time," in which case the parents feel relief that they have caught it in time, or "I only took a little," which makes parents feel grateful that the experimentation caused no serious damage. That's the reaction kids bank on. Unfortunately, kids are usually lying.

Kids caught at school give very predictable responses: "Somebody must have put it in my locker." "A kid asked me to hold it for him." "I didn't know what it was." These are usually lies, also.

Knowing that you may not get the true picture makes it even more important that you act carefully. Here are a few guidelines.

1. Pick a time and place where you will not be interrupted. Expect to be an interrogator who has to extract answers. Expect reluctance, evasiveness, and flashes of anger, but be persistent. This initial session will largely determine your course of action.

2. Don't let anger interfere. If wrath and punishment greet every disclosure, any kid will clam up. Cork your anger and keep it corked. Stay calm and ask for the substance, the amount, the time of day, the location, the source, and the associates. Try to get the entire story from beginning until right now. Details are important, as you will see later. Assume this is not the first episode.

3. Pledge that you will keep confidential any names that your child reveals and keep that pledge. The greatest sin among teenagers is to 'rat' on someone else, so don't press hard on this issue. This is not the best time to take on the problems of additional kids.

4. Emphasize the importance of getting the entire true story now. The child's abuse has damaged the trust between you, and if your child holds back now, you have lost your best shot at the truth. Explain that this is the time for honesty, not maneuvering or negotiating.

5. Don't talk about punishments or penalties at this point. You are not prepared to decide upon your approach yet. Don't answer hypothetical questions like, "What would you do if I told you that . . .?" Deal only in the facts of the case now.

6. Have a second, separate session a day or two later. Explain that you want to be certain that you have the correct version, and ask for a repeat of the details. This is simply a check on accuracy, so watch for discrepancies from the original version.

After digesting these two sessions, review any past incidents or warning signs that have aroused your suspicions in the past. Here's where the written record suggested in Chapter Three may help. You also may want to check with your key people who may add more information. Finally, if you can check out any factual details of the story with others, do so.

These tactics may seem harsh—more like grilling a criminal than questioning one of your children. But remember that this is a crucial point, a point at which it's essential that you understand if a progression is under way.

HANDLING EXPERIMENTATION

If you believe that your youngster confessed the entire story, and all other information validates that conclusion, you, as a parent, probably can proceed without professional help. As a precaution you may want to consult someone experienced in teenage chemical abuse to give you reassurance and to verify your preliminary diagnosis.

If the use is minimal and in the beginning stages, your first step is a commitment to abstain. Don't underestimate the power of your influence as a parent. Years of loving, nurturing, caring, and teaching have built up a reservoir of debt in your youngster. That's the reason that they feel guilty when they disobey. Almost all kids need and want parental approval, though it may not always be evident. This is the best time for you to play your trump card. Later it will be far less effective.

Do not debate any facet of the problem. Insist on a commitment to abstinence for these important reasons:

1. Using has the potential to start a dangerous progression.

2. Using risks problems with police and school.

3. Using adds unnecessary tension, conflict, and worry to a family.

If your youngster makes the commitment, you may want to discuss how he or she will stay clean, deal with user friends, and abstain at parties. If you feel inadequate for that kind of discussion, you may want to suggest a visit to a counselor who has experience in helping kids return to straight behavior. It may be wise to find a support group of teenagers who are all ex-users. Remember that the longer they have used, the tougher it is for them to stop. If your child is clearly an experimenter only, these suggestions may not be appropriate.

AN EXTREME RESPONSE

Karen's father was a strict teetotaler who had grown up with an alcoholic father. He carried powerful emotions about alcohol and when Karen, then sixteen, came home

New Year's Eve smelling of alcohol, he hit the roof and created an uproar. About a year later, Karen came home from her waitressing job with liquor on her breath. Her father exploded, saying that if she planned to drink she would have to move out; he refused to let her live at home and drink. The mother interceded and suggested that the ultimatum was too extreme—that other family members were entitled to voice their views as well. Father reconsidered and agreed that his should not be the only voice considered. Then he added, "It may not be fair to force you out; it's your home, too. But if you plan to live at home and drink, I must move out." He sounded melodramatic but he was clearly sincere. When the dust cleared, Karen had agreed not to drink while she was living at home.

This extreme response illustrates several points. On the one hand, the father showed that he would go to any length to stop the drinking, a very powerful and clear message. He was lucky that his ultimatum worked because he had made several serious mistakes. First, by reacting emotionally he didn't have time to think through a more reasonable response. He also didn't give his wife time to react; so they had no chance to present a unified approach. Finally, by issuing an ultimatum, he had painted himself into a corner whereby his daughter could have forced him out of his own home.

There are better ways to respond.

FORGIVE BUT DON'T FORGET

Until now we are assuming that your child has been cooperative and is sincere about the commitment. You can afford a soft approach because you believe in your child; by giving the problem back, you have shown your trust along with your initial disapproval. This allows your child the opportunity to take a major step toward self-responsibility. But don't sit back smugly and think your job is over; you must continue to keep your eyes wide open.

With the commitment goes the understanding that a relapse means an automatic referral for a professional evaluation (more about evaluation later) and some lost privileges at home. At this stage parents must begin walking that careful line between vigilance, which is essential, and harassment, which is constant questioning and double checking. Hopefully your trust will be rewarded; but if it isn't, be relentless about keeping your promises and act immediately.

THE QUESTION OF INCENTIVES

One family never regretted a plan that they used with each of their four children. When each child entered junior high, their parents offered them a deal. In their community it was a ritual for seniors to take a vacation trip during spring break. The seniors banded together and headed for the sun. The deal was this. In exchange for being alcohol- and drug-free throughout secondary school, the family would rent a condo in Florida for a week and the senior could invite three friends. The rest of the family stayed home. A second part of the bargain was that any slipup during school not only cancelled the condo trip but also cancelled any senior trip at all.

The terms worked beautifully for all four kids, and the idea has spread in the community. The children had a special reason to say NO because their senior trip was at stake. Since the condo rental also counted as a graduation present it wasn't as extravagant as it sounds. The parents were aware that four teenagers away from home represented total freedom and a huge temptation to run wild, but so far that hasn't happened. In return this couple reaped some precious, worry-free years.

An incentive doesn't have to be costly or flamboyant. It can be an agreement guaranteeing the use of the family car whenever it is not in use by adults; a rising allowance with each 'clean' year; an agreement to throw and host several teenage parties a year; or any other exchange that will sweeten the pot.

If it suits your family's value system, this might be the time for exchanging a special incentive for honoring the commitment.

SUMMARY

When you find evidence of abuse:

1. Take no action until you are calm emotionally and have agreed with your spouse regarding which action to take.

2. Sit quietly with your youngster and try to get all the details of the incident. If possible, check out the story with another source.

3. Review any warning signs or suspicious incidents from the past.

4. If your diagnosis is use in its early stages, put parental pressure on for a commitment to stop, including the actions you will take if the youngster breaks the commitment.

5. Consider offering an incentive to abstain.

6. Offer counseling or a support group if it seems appropriate.

7. Continue to be vigilant.

Chapter Seven

Tougher Cases

Many parents aren't so lucky in discovering use in the experimental stage and in getting full cooperation. If the evidence that you collect is full of evasions, contradictions, and incomplete answers, you can assume the damage is greater than it appears. Evasiveness and limited disclosure clearly mean that there is more to hide, requiring you to take a more aggressive approach.

HOW BAD IS IT?

The most significant element in the puzzle is the extent of the use—very elusive information. Since you are certain that your child is not being completely open, you can anticipate one of two behaviors: open defiance or pretending to be clean. When youngsters are using at a level that they feel they can handle, their style will normally be to use as quietly as possible, claiming they have stopped, and try to convince you that you can relax. Some teenagers put drugs and alcohol in the same category with sex—an exciting, forbidden discovery that delivers loads of pleasure with no consequences. They are wrong on both counts, but they are always convinced that they can personally beat the odds.

A user like Dave, in Chapter One, can carry on the charade for a long time by being careful, showing a cooperative attitude, and explaining away the suspicions of parents. Lack of clear-cut evidence that using is causing negative side effects weakens your case, but not hopelessly so; you simply follow a different tack. The time has probably come to request a profe sional evaluation by a chemical dependency counselor.

EVALUATION

One method of evaluation is an interview by an experienced counselor who tries to get a true picture of your youngster's use/abuse history. Sometimes the interview includes family members. The more information that the family can provide to the interviewer, the more accurate the evaluation. A common ploy is to try to "con" the evaluator. Many evaluators, however, are ex-abusers who have traveled the road themselves, and all evaluators are familiar with *denial, minimizing, evasion*, and other attempts at deception.

The skill of the evaluator is critical because most of the clients are, at best, reluctant witnesses at their own trial. Good evaluators have an instinct which helps them form a valid picture, even from partial or inaccurate information. Their findings, especially if they recommend further evaluation or treatment, should be heeded as the voice of experience. Sometimes the results will be that the interview was a total con and no recommendation can be made. That is usually a sign that you need to use more aggressive approaches; subsequent chapters cover these approaches.

A second evaluation method involves staying in a treatment facility for at least a few days. Obviously this allows greater opportunity to break down the client and obtain the truth. Common techniques are one-on-one sessions with a counselor or psychologist plus group sessions with peers. The peer sessions are often very fruitful because other kids are adept at puncturing the facade of a conning contemporary.

You are under no obligation to follow the recommendations of an evaluation. It's important to emphasize this to youngsters who are frightened by the possibility that an unfamiliar professional may force them into treatment or brand them as a mental case. The family will decide the next step. The evaluation is another piece of the picture, this time provided by an objective professional. However, ignoring recommendations should be done with great care.

Let's assume that the evaluator reports that the interview failed because your youngster was dishonest, uncooperative, resentful, or whatever. This usually means a kid who doesn't want to quit. Immediately you are in a much more serious situation. The same is true if the evaluator recommends further evaluation or treatment and you get a refusal. Some parents throw up their hands and hope for the best; others try to force treatment on their child (which sometimes turns out to be successful); and some continue to search for a solution within the family resources. Your approach will depend on your energy, your patience, and your personal style of parenting.

If a professional evaluation can't be arranged, or if the evaluation seems invalid, you have several other avenues to pursue. A self-survey is a good place to begin.

A SIMPLE BAROMETER

Teenagers begin using with the unshakable confidence that they can handle it; they don't like any information that challenges that confidence. They rarely admit that they are losing control. They habitually minimize the true extent of their use to quiet the still, small warnings that are usually just below the surface of their minds. They reassure themselves by setting limits that separate them from true abusers—or so they think. What they don't realize is how their limits keep changing to match the level of use. They make promises to themselves such as, "I never buy it; I only use when someone gives it to me" or "I never drink during the week" or "I never plan to do it." As time goes on, the user breaks these promises and sets new limits, such as, "I only spend five dollars per week" or "I never drink alone" or "I only use when it's safe; never when I'm driving."

As the progression continues, the personal limits escalate so that the abuser can hold on to the illusion of being in control. The quiz that follows, if answered honestly, will indicate if use is escalating and if control is becoming more difficult.

Try to encourage honest answers, but don't be surprised if your youngster tries to laugh off these questions as totally irrelevant. Abusers don't like self-examination and bristle at the suggestion that they may be losing control. Leave the questions with your child even if the youngster refuses to answer them; a truism in adolescent treatment is that good information never goes to waste. It may lie dormant for a time but may surface later when doubts began to gather. The decision to stop using often comes from an accumulation of negative side effects and growing doubts.

DEPENDENCY QUIZ

1. Am I using more often?

2. Have I increased the amount or potency?

3. Do I break promises to myself? (only three beers tonight)

4. Have I ever passed out while using?

5. Have I ever been unable to remember afterward what happened while I was using?

6. Have I ever been embarrassed later by what I did while using?

7. Has using caused trouble with friends, family, school, or police?

8. Have others shown concern about my use?

9. Do I ever worry about my use?

Obviously, "yes" answers are the wrong answers.

CONTRACTS

Again you should arrange a quiet, uninterrupted session where you can explain your views and set some conditions. Make it clear that you will not tolerate occasional use, casual use, controlled use, safe use, or any use at all. You want abstinence until the your child reaches legal age; compromises do not interest you. State up front that the teenager has not convinced you that use has stopped; that you think that it is continuing because the youngster thinks that there is no real danger. Admit that even though your teenager may not be worried, you are. Say that you want to trust your child and that you don't want to follow him or her around and play detective. Instead you want an understanding that, if use continues, there will be consequences. Since the child claims to have stopped, ask the child to enter a contract with you to show good faith. Here is a sample contract:

> I,_____ , pledge that I will neither possess nor use alcohol or drugs in any form until I have reached legal age. I understand that breaking this contract will be interpreted as proof that I am unable to stop without help. Therefore I will do what my parents think is appropriate, even if it means entering a residential treatment program.
>
> Witnessed by _____ Date_____

A contract like this raises the stakes for a youngster who wants to keep using but pretends not to be doing so. The added pressure may tip the scales toward quitting or cutting back. From your viewpoint the contract means that you have laid the groundwork for action of your choosing since it contains an admission that the youngster needs help, a key step in any recovery program.

If you can't get a signature on the contract, there is a strong possibility that dependency is already so entrenched that the adolescent is afraid to make the commitment.

OUTSIDE SUPPORT

A second approach is to suggest attendance at a support group for kids who have stopped using and are trying to stay straight. These groups help members by discussing their feelings, their temptations, and their daily ups and downs. The common goal of remaining clean lends strength to all members as they see others face the same problems and succeed. These groups are also quick to spot a fraud and quickly straighten out anyone who tries to "do a number" on them. School counselors usually know how to contact these groups.

Another source of help is counseling sessions that work on helping kids make the transition back to a straight life. Any trained counselor knows how to offer support and encouragement, how to listen to frustration and guilt, and how to make practical suggestions that will eliminate some of the trouble spots.

At any point in the progression you can suggest *Alcoholic Anonymous*, an organization listed in almost every telephone book. Many local chapters set up groups exclusively for teenagers who are trying to recover from alcohol or chemical abuse. The reputation of AA is as solid as a rock.

BLANKET REFUSALS

The options in this chapter are reasonable ones for a youngster who has either given up using or is operating at a minimal level. Refusing to cooperate with any of them may suggest that your child will not allow any barriers between him or her and the abuse. If that is true, it means dependence is so serious that you are now dealing with an abuser.

SUMMARY

When you are certain of prolonged use:

1. Arrange an evaluation by a professional dependency counselor.

2. Present the *Dependency Quiz*.

3. Insist on a signed contract.

4. Offer a support group or counseling.

Chapter Eight

A Fallback Position

If your home is one of those in which you have used all the arguments, pleas, and threats that you can, and the subject of teenage use remains at a stalemate, you may decide to adopt a fallback position. Though you may have written a near-perfect script for your children, there is no guarantee that they will play the parts the way that you wrote them.

There is a common scenario in which teenagers use alcohol and/or drugs at a level that they claim is practically harmless. These are not belligerent, defiant, out-of-control teenagers. They believe that they will never be caught up in abuse, and they dismiss the legality problem as inconsequential. They simply don't buy the risk factor. The rest of their conduct as sons or daughters is relatively trouble-free.

These kids don't want to be hypocritical or deceitful about their use, nor do their parents want them to be. Yet how can parents cope—by ignoring, accepting, condoning? It is an awkward and delicate situation that poses a different problem and requires different tactics. It's a case where you choose not to allow the tree to obscure the forest and jeopardize an otherwise satisfactory family relationship. Far from a cave-in, you maintain certain rules and stand ready to intervene if the situation deteriorates. First, let's consider a broader perspective, the myth of parental control.

WHEN VALUES COLLIDE

Have you ever wished you could take your kids to dog obedience school where they would learn to sit, heel, fetch, and behave on your command? You would have complete control and be the ultimate authority. Have you ever wondered why your kids don't always accept your advice, respect your opinions, or allow you to make their big decisions for them?

Most parents do not control their kids; at best, most parents exert their influence through personal example and by gradually revealing the personal value system that governs their lives. But no matter how influential you may be and how sound, practical, and rewarding your value system may be, your kids may still choose to follow their own, different values.

Does this mean that you are a weak, irresponsible, and ineffective parent? No! It means that "generation gap" is not just a clever term. Almost all children drift outside the parameters parents have tried to set. Most kids prefer to test the world for themselves and come to independent conclusions, especially when the generations appear to be out of step with one another.

THE GREAT DIVIDE

A value collision in a household requires some fancy footwork to limit rather that escalate the conflict. A parent fighting for control pitted against a teenager fighting for independence can transform a home into a battle zone. An issue, highly important to both parties, can build a wall that stops all communications—not only on that issue but on all issues. When anger, tension, and hostility dominate a home, nobody wins. If that situation is shaping up in your home, please accept the responsibility for taking the initiative to defuse it. After all, as a mature adult, yours is the greater obligation.

SEPARATING THE ISSUES

As an illustration, let's assume that your seventeen-year-old child has made it evident that alcohol is no longer a taboo. This disappoints you because, on the premise that "If they don't get wet, they can't drown," you were hoping for a totally dry response. A closer analysis reveals that your clean-slate ideal was actually an insurance policy against your real fears, which are not of the "Lips that touch liquor shall never touch mine" mentality. Instead, they are the genuine fears of the possible consequences.

The real fear is not that drinking will instantaneously doom teenagers; it is that drinking exposes them to the possibilities of:

- becoming a victim of chemicals and their deadly progression
- driving while high or with those who are high

- running afoul of school or legal penalties

- neglecting schoolwork, job, or other responsibilities

This list may not be complete; you may want to add other concerns. Nothing on the list is absolutely inevitable. Examine each fear and consider a checkpoint or a process that would give you some assurance that these serious consequences are not a factor. Putting together some assurances is impossible without cooperation from your teenager, and that is why communications cannot be allowed to rupture. Your position is not that you approve or accept the situation, but that you can tolerate it better if you know that there are safeguards in place that will allow you to sleep a little easier.

A DISCLAIMER OF SORTS

The options suggested here should not be interpreted as accepting teenager using—they are intended to try to cut the losses in an undesirable situation. To emphasize the point, make it clear that your kids cannot expect the same kind of moral, financial, or emotional support they receive when they face other problems. If they decide to override parental guidelines and plunge into the adult world, they must accept the responsibility that goes with the territory.

Finally, if you feel that any of these actions compromise your principles and put you in the position of making it easier for kids to use, please follow your instincts. This is a sensitive area and you must decide upon your personal course.

POLITICS AT HOME

Politics is sometimes called the art of the possible. At this point, whatever is possible is the key to your negotiations with your teenagers. Assuming you have maintained a fertile atmosphere for communications and cooperation and you have calmly stated your real fears, you can suggest some benchmarks, safeguards, or warning signs—whatever you choose to call them.

For example, the truest indicators of alcoholic progression are frequency and amount. Measuring progression requires that someone monitor drinking habits and keep some sort of record. In an ideal world your teenager would admit in advance when he plans to drink and be willing to disclose afterward what and how much he drank or keep a written diary, similar to calorie counting, which would reveal signs of progression. Neither is very likely to happen. In reality parents will most likely be responsible for the monitoring based on information that they can gather.

Consider a trade-off similar to this example.

Parents will agree to:

1. not hassle the chemical issue

2. not play detective by constant questioning

3. provide a safe-ride-home arrangement

Teenagers will agree to:

1. stop using if negative side effects begin to appear
2. accept all responsibilities, including financial, that arise from chemicals

3. answer questions about chemicals truthfully

A LITMUS TEST

One characteristic of users is their inability to diagnose their progression. They can see it in the lives of others but not in their own lives. It's not unusual for students to describe concern for a friend who appears to be using at the danger point while their own use is in essence the same. But they will deny that they personally have the same problem as their friend.

Explain that the youngster must guard against such self-deception. Suggest that the teenager answer the following questions periodically; they are accurate indicators of trouble.

1. Do I sometimes avoid social events without chemicals in favor of those with chemicals?

2. Are chemicals changing my social life or my friends?

3. Do I look forward to using the same way I do to a date, a concert, or a pizza?

4. Am I using more frequently or in larger quantities?

AUTOS AND CHEMICALS

Teenagers, chemicals, and automobiles can be handled by an agreement beforehand. Part of it should be that the adolescent will never request the use of family automobiles when chemicals are to be consumed, and under no circumstances will he or she drive the family autos after using. If you get resistance on this one, reemphasize the fact that there is already one legal problem: the drinking age.

The second part of the agreement should be some version of the safe-ride-home program mentioned in Chapter Three. A warning: It is one thing to provide transportation for your own child after some drinking but quite another to tote home friends who have been drinking. Think twice before accepting passengers unless they are stone sober. Consider what you would be thinking if another parent dropped off your teenager in those circumstances.

AVOIDING TROUBLE

Two factors that bring using teenagers and the authorities together are location and noise. The classic combination is a horde of teenagers gathered in a park, beach, vacant lot, or abandoned building late at night with plenty of alcohol, drugs, and a booming sound system.

To most teenagers loud music and a noisy crowd are an unbeatable combination. The alcohol and drugs, almost always present, are an accepted part of that scene. Some kids get totally blasted, and some don't drink at all; but all are at risk if it comes down to police intervention. Avoiding a bust means knowing when to leave a party—even a party at its peak. Since drinking and using is only part of the mix of dancing, listening, and socializing, discuss with your kids the best way to participate without being in the wrong place at the wrong time.

These are intervention buttons for the police:

- heavy traffic, especially fast or reckless driving

- house parties that spill out onto the lawn or street

- complaining phone calls from neighbors

- destruction of property, public or private

- uninvited guests

Provided your kids are sober, they should be able to sense when parties are going over the edge and clear out before someone calls the authorities. It requires common sense and willpower to leave a party before it's over.

Visibility is also crucial. At a house party celebrating the end of a successful soccer season, several athletes were drinking beer—some in the house, some in the basement, and some on the front lawn while playing croquet. The front lawn was in full view of the neighbors and passing automobile traffic. Sure enough, the school got many telephone calls, and questioned the athletes about the party. Those who admitted they were drinking lost their eligibility; those who lied about it did not receive penalties. This is a messy story for many reasons. Some drinkers were not punished because they were either discreet or dishonest—not because they were innocent. It was too tempting for some of those athletes, and they set aside their integrity to save their skin. That's called adding one mistake to another and doesn't do much for moral fiber. So it goes when you travel the wrong roads.

CHIPPERS

A teenager who uses drugs, maintaining that drug use is harmless, presents an even nastier problem. Parents who try to delay the start of drinking do so knowing that when their child reaches legal age, the rules change. But street drugs are illegal at every age.

"Chipper" is a term used for people who use drugs infrequently and occasionally. They often claim to be the equivalent of social drinkers because they are not dependent, their use does not escalate, and they truly could quit if they so chose. It is possible for chippers to remain at their level, sometimes called a recreational level, for years without negative effects.

This information is not meant to diminish the dangers described elsewhere in this book or to encourage parents to accept drug use. The point is that parents can find themselves living with a chipper. When drug use isn't causing other visible problems, parents' objections can center only on legality and the risk factor.

Knowing that a resourceful teenager can conceal drug use from parents, try extra hard to avoid a stalemate that stops communication. After constantly hearing parents' warnings about the dangers of drug use, teenagers often simply ignore the warnings (which they don't believe anyway), avoid the subject, and close off communications with their parents. The parents become adversaries and, if a teenager does begin to worry about being out of control, it's unlikely that the parents will be told.

Begin by discussing your fears, which probably include:

- the risk of drug dependency

- the danger of taking contaminated drugs

- trouble with school or police

- associating with unsavory, law-breaking companions

If your teenager is honest and sincere (although most drug users act very guardedly), try to get some agreement about what would be the signals that chipping is turning into dependency. The same signs as for alcohol would apply: declining grades at school, preoccupations with drugs, escalation in use, and so forth. Make it clear that you will watch for those warning signs and expect to be able to discuss them. Insist that YOU will decide when the red flag is showing and, if there is disagreement between you, let a professional evaluation decide.

Meanwhile strive for an attitude that shows care and concern without harping or lecturing. Pressure on the teenager to go straight can be applied without shouting, arguments, or snide remarks. One way is to set up some house rules, one of which should absolutely prohibit drugs or drug paraphernalia in your home. If your child brings them home, destroy them. You wouldn't allow stolen property in your house and you shouldn't allow street drugs.

As with alcohol use, accept no responsibility for problems arising from drug use. That means no bailouts, no loans, no straightening out drug-related messes, and no providing alibis or excuses when trouble arises. The only exception would be if there is a need for treatment.

If you have other children in the house you would be wise to guard against contamination. Keeping all drugs out of the house is a good start, but try to get a commitment from your teenager that no introductions will be made to the other children. There are many cases of older siblings, able to control their own use and confident of their worldly experience, who have started younger brothers and sisters on drugs. Unfortunately they learned too late that their siblings didn't practice the same restraint. If you want to see a family turn against one of their own, visit a home where a young victim, badly messed up by drugs, was started down the road by an older brother or sister who intended only a harmless initation. They thought it was an act of comradeship to teach the young ones the ropes. Too often it backfires and family life explodes.

THE CHIPPER'S CODE

Nobody knows how many chippers are operating in our society. We do know that staying clear of serious trouble requires self-discipline, not only in steadfastly limiting drug use but in avoiding the pitfalls that accompany a secretive walk through a drug world dominated by a criminal subculture. There is little data on chippers because they don't appear in clinics or treatment centers unless they have lost control and moved into progression. Obviously chippers are not immune forever just because they manage to contain their use for a time. It is dangerous, especially for teenagers who already believe themselves invulnerable, to believe that it is safe to be a chipper.

Chippers avoid junkie behavior by following self-imposed limits and can restrict their exposure by following self-protective patterns. Their self-discipline is their armor. These rules, common to many chippers, are not listed here to show teenagers a safe way to use, but to show what chippers believe they must do to maintain control. Contrarily, teenagers who cannot hold to restrictions like these are very much at risk, whether they admit it or not.

1. Stick to limits of frequency and amount.

2. Never mix or change drugs.

3. Never use with strangers or in public.

4. Always buy from the same source.

5. Never buy large quantities or go into debt to a dealer.

6. Never deal.

WHERE WILL IT ALL END?

It's almost easier to take a hard-line position against teenage use of drugs or alcohol than to try to find a fallback position that you can endure. Tolerating behavior that clashes with your beliefs requires a ton of restraint and is often a ticket to a stress trip.

Yet it's a universal truth for parents that alienating your children is devastating to everyone. Rancor and bitterness will put a sour taste into all aspects of life. Parents must walk a tightrope, balancing what they want with what they get. The secret may be to let the pressure of your convictions, which you need not sacrifice, work while you try to stay alert to serious danger. Meanwhile, do what you can to reduce the risk and wait. Wait with the knowledge that with your help your kids will turn out OK.

SUMMARY

1. Don't allow disagreements to interrupt communication—keep on talking.

2. Explain your real fears frankly.

3. Work out agreements such as promising:

   a. no nagging or lecturing
   b. a safe ride home
   c. no playing detective

   in exchange for:

   a. being honest about chemical use
   b. accepting total responsibility
   c. promising to quit if warning signs appear

4. Encourage use of a self-survey as a monitoring tool.

5. Discuss how to avoid situations that invite legal trouble.

6. Insist on an evaluation when things get out of hand.

7. Don't allow drugs or paraphernalia in your home.

8. Discuss and guard against contamination of other siblings.

9. Discuss characteristics that separate chippers from abusers.

Chapter Nine

Entrenched Abuse

$\mathbf{P}$arents usually have trouble admitting that a child of theirs has become a serious abuser, one who is unwilling to quit. There is no possibility of moving forward until you can accept that diagnosis and switch gears to a level that matches the abuse. If you cling to the hope that the next promise, in a string of broken promises, will be kept; that the next phony excuse, in a series of phony excuses, will turn out to be true; that the next time your teenager gets in trouble, after many times, will be the one that turns him or her around, you are not acting as a parent. You are acting as an accomplice.

A real roadblock to acknowledging that you have an abusing child is the connotation that many of us attach to anyone who can't control a habit—that it is a sign of weakness of character. That belief assumes that the person could stop if he or she really wanted to. Classifying abuse as a disease, as most treatment facilities do, has the advantage of making it more palatable for everyone. It subtly shifts the responsibility for the problem from the moral fiber of the person to the onset of a disease and confers patient status on what some people label as irresponsible behavior.

Despite how you personally classify abuse, dealing with it in your home usually means a nightmare. Abusers who resist all efforts to help them are destructive forces in a family. The destruction can be psychological, as the relationships in the family deteriorate under the pressure. It also can be physical, ranging from sleepless nights to physical harm as rows and arguments get violent.

Each family has a breaking point, and it isn't always visible at the beginning of the campaign. The uproar, the worry, the constant concern and preoccupation about what should be done, and the anger and guilt all take a heavy toll, literally tearing families apart.

SUPPORT FOR THE INNOCENT

If this scenario happens in your family, the first thing that you should do is probably the last thing you'd think of —get some help for the rest of the family. This can be handled by meeting with trained counselors or joining a support group. Parents with no outlet other than family members frequently hash and rehash the problem until they feel like they are devouring each other. It is hard to agree on what to do next, and it is easy to start blaming each other. Siblings often get entangled in the controversy, struggling with divided loyalties, or they simply get pushed aside and ignored as the family concentrates on the abuser.

The innocent are doing the suffering, and that is unacceptable. Make some contacts for any family member who needs help, and try hard to keep the rest of the family healthy. Without some outside support and reassurance it's easy to let this one problem dominate the family until the frustration and feelings of inadequacy are overwhelming. The result can be an unhappy, unhealthy family.

THE WELL-MEANING ACCOMPLICE

It took years of observation, mostly of alcoholics and their families, to realize that abusers have a way of manipulating others into playing supporting roles that contribute to the continuation of abuse. Parents of youngsters in treatment are astonished to learn how they inadvertently made it easier for their child to continue using. The natural parental tendency to protect and help plays right into the abuser's need for someone to run interference and to compensate for gaps that are appearing in the abuser's responsibilities. Following are some common responses that actually contribute to abuse.

Denial

Denying the seriousness and extent of the problem is one way some families try to keep the family self-respect intact. They make statements such as, "He's just raising hell like I did" or "All kids try drugs; she's no different" or "At least the school hasn't thrown him out like his friend George" or "She'll snap out of it once she gets out of school." Repeating statements like these, even if you don't believe them, is comforting and helps maintain the illusion that soon all will be well. But you should realize that it's the same illusion the abuser embraces so desperately.

Denial also sends a clear message to your child that you are willing to live with the status quo. That message alone neutralizes any serious attempts you might make to stop the abuse.

Enabling

If denial is a sin of omission, enabling is a sin of commission. Instead of attacking the problem, the family makes adjustments to cut down the conflict and turmoil so that life can continue to run smoothly. Anyone who doesn't allow the abuser to bear the responsibility for the abuse is an enabler. In family treatment, counselors often have to explain how well-meaning family members were unknowingly acting like coconspirators.

These are examples of enabling behavior.

1. A mother calls school to say her daughter is sick when she is really hungover.

2. A father pays to fix a car damaged by a son's drunk driving.

3. A younger sister hides drug paraphernalia in her room so the folks won't find it, and her sister can say, "I told you that I quit; go ahead and search my room if you want."

4. An older married brother allows his brother to sleep at his house rather than going home bombed.

5. Another student feeds answers in an exam to a girl who got stoned the day before and didn't study.

6. A buddy organizes other party-goers to chip in for damages when a drunken friend angrily trashes a friend's family room because his girlfriend left the party in disgust.

Giving In

In some families, peace and harmony are the first priorities. Rather than confront an abusing child, this family will make outrageous adjustments to avoid a scene. Once the abuser has the upper hand and can control the family, usually by being unpleasant or belligerent, any effort by the family to try to help the abuser is doomed to fail. The youngster runs wild, and the family suffers in silence, preferring peace to taking an action that might be upsetting.

Codependency

Codependency is the act of shaping one's behavior to the needs of an abuser. This can be an illness of its own when the need to complement the life of an abuser overrides one's sense of reality. An example is someone who takes on the role of a martyr. This person responds to the selfish, ungrateful behavior of the abuser by remaining steadfast and responsible through it all, without taking any action to stop it. The nastier and more despicable the abuser becomes, the greater the martyrdom. Not only is this the wrong road to sainthood, but also it is a destructive attitude for both parties.

Martyrdom is not the only form of codependence. You should consult with an experienced counselor to be certain that neither you nor any family member is inadvertently playing into the hands of the abuser.

RAISING THE BOTTOM

If you have taken steps to protect the rest of the family and are certain that you are not aiding and abetting the abuser, you can focus on several courses of action aimed at helping the abuser stop.

Most dependency counselors will agree that the best client is one who has volunteered to accept help. Often the abuser reaches the point when he or she hits bottom. Life becomes so unpleasant and unrewarding that defeat and fear become dominant. The abuser finally realizes that he or she is clearly losing the battle with abuse. The only trouble is that watching that process and waiting for the bottom is perdition itself. But the process can sometimes be speeded up. Abusers require a certain comfort level or the pressure becomes too great and they cave in.

It's possible for a family to "raise the bottom" by carefully lowering the comfort level so that life is not so easy for the abuser. Take the position that your youngster has forfeited the fringe benefits that go with family life because choosing to continue abusing is contrary to the family values. Depending on your judgment and imagination this can mean no financial support, no use of family vehicles, no laundry service, no cleaning of the abuser's room, no meals except at mealtime, curfew at ten o'clock, or any other possibilities that make sense at your house.

Psychologically your position should be that you are eager and willing to help put Humpty Dumpty together again but only on your terms. Loving the abuser while hating the abuse is a very tough number but that's what you must try to do. Remind the abuser that while he or she chooses to continue, you cannot pretend that all is well; stopping is the only move that will set things right again.

Your disapproval plus the reduction of creature comforts are reminders that the life of an abuser is not that sweet. Make sure the abuser knows that your door remains unlocked but that he or she must open it.

INTERVENTION

A technique that can tip the scales for an abuser is a process called intervention. It is difficult and requires the help of an experienced counselor. The counselor arranges a meeting of the key people in the abuser's life—family, friends, employer, teachers—all those who have a sincere desire to help the abuser change his or her life. No one informs the abuser ahead of time; he or she is brought to the meeting to hear those who care describe their concern.

Several ingredients are essential. Incidents and details of abuse must be included so that the variety and volume of the incidents are simply too overwhelming to deny. Everyone also must explain how the abuse is changing the relationship, and what that person feels he or she must do if the abuser refuses the offer of help.

For example, a boyfriend might say:

"Every party we've gone to lately, including last
Saturday night, has been spoiled because all you want
to do is get high. And when you do, you're no fun. You
change, and you're not the same girl; you don't talk
sense and the other kids know it; they're calling you a
pothead. I spend half the evening worrying about what
you'll do next and the other half trying to get you in
shape to go home. You keep promising that you'll stop
but I don't believe you anymore. If you cared about us,
the two of us, you'd get some help and until you do I
give up. I still care but I'm not going out with you while
you use, it's just no good."

Or, a father might say:

"Four times since school started you've come home
after curfew woozy—drunk or high, it doesn't matter
which. Your grades are lower than ever, and I'm
ashamed of the way you talk back to your mother and
me—like that argument we had Sunday night when you
used words we never use in our home. You've changed
and I believe it's because of drugs or booze or both.
Either you can't or you won't stop—I don't care
because this cannot go on. Instead of being proud of
you I find myself angry. I wonder if this will ever end,
and I wait for the day when you're old enough to leave
home and be on your own. Our family has become so
unhappy over this issue that if you won't accept help,
we are going to find another place for you to live."

As these examples show, intervention brings out
powerful emotions and can be very traumatic for everyone.

That's why it's wise to have an experienced professional present to keep things in perspective. The object is to bombard the abuser with confrontation from so many people that he or she can no longer deny the pain the abuse is causing others.

An ideal intervention is when the abuser leaves the meeting and is taken directly to a treatment facility where the parents have prearranged admission. When the abuser stalls about accepting treatment but promises to stop, the jury is still out. It is vital that those at the meeting do not renege on their promises or the abuser will return to his or her merry ways, secure in the knowledge that things aren't really that bad; the abuser has then managed to sabotage the intervention. But if everyone sticks to their guns and their promises, they have contributed to raising the bottom, and the intervention may work.

Well-planned interventions will always depend on the state of mind of the abusers, but they should never be considered a failure because abuse doesn't stop immediately. Hopefully the love and concern shown at the intervention will continue to work, and the evidence will force the abusers to admit what they are doing to themselves.

THROWING THEM OUT

The most dramatic response to an abusing teenager who won't stop is to file an incorrigibility complaint with legal officials and have the abuser removed from your home to a detention center, a treatment facility, or a foster home. The process is not a simple one and conditions at home must be extremely bad—both for you to make the request and for a court to take action. It begins with a report to the local police station. This usually happens when the abuser has been physically violent or has stolen repeatedly from the family, but those are not the only grounds for incorrigibility. Setting this process in motion is often the final step in the progression of raising the bottom to the point where the abuser accepts help.

An eighteen-year-old boy named Roger had been terrorizing his family for almost four years when his parents finally decided to take legal action against him. He was a heavy-duty abuser of both drugs and alcohol and was drunk or high almost all the time. During four years of sporadic attendance at high school he had attained the status only of a first-semester junior. He had been arrested three times, once each for shoplifting, speeding, and attempted burglary; but he had somehow kept himself out of jail, partly because of his parents' intervention. He had stolen money from the family, refused to follow any reasonable house rules, and physically threatened his mother.

For years the parents vacillated between getting tough and giving him another chance. Finally they petitioned for and got a court order that kept Roger off their home premises. They changed the locks on the doors after a burglary because they believed that he had been the burglar.

Over the next two years they saw their son only occasionally, mostly when he needed money, which they always refused, and sometimes when he vowed to straighten out. After one of these visits he convinced them that he was serious, and they allowed him to come home. He enrolled in college and for the past two years has been working part-time and attending school regularly, receiving decent grades. He is no longer rebellious, and life at home is normal. He never undertook any formal counseling or treatment; it simply took him a long time to realize that his abusing life was a waste. He admits that his parents were absolutely correct in throwing him out; in fact, he insists that they should have done it sooner.

The point of this story is not that there is a happy ending. The point is that the parents finally asserted their right to have a normal life and refused to let their son continue to spoil it. Roger was contaminating the entire family, dominating it with his abusing behavior, and there really was no alternative but to get him out of the house. It took courage and determination for the parents to take that action, but when they did, they knew immediately that they had done the right thing.

A less extreme alternative than legal action is shipping kids off to a relative or trusted friend who is willing to fight the battle for a while. The change may not interrupt the abuse, but it makes a clear statement and provides relief for the family.

Any action a family takes can turn out to be the one that results in the decision to ask for help. There is seldom a way to know in advance what it will take to make the abuser give in; that's why every approach must be tried.

SUMMARY

When you are certain of entrenched abuse and are getting very little cooperation:

1. Arrange for counseling or support groups for family members if they need it.

2. Figure out, perhaps with the help of a counselor, whether any family members are inadvertently contributing to the abuse.

3. Make a plan to reduce the abuser's comfort level by raising the bottom.

4. Arrange an intervention.

5. Keep the pressure on to enter treatment.

6. Consider moving the abuser out of the household.

Chapter Ten

Therapy and Treatment

A special report to the United States Congress in 1987 identified certain recommended components for a successful chemical dependency recovery program. Among these are:

Detox - insuring that the client has no access to drugs or alcohol during therapy. The belief is that the body must be clear of toxins before effective treatment can occur.

Behavior - helping the client understand his or her behavior—self-control, social skills, and coping mechanisms

Counseling - increasing understanding about self-perception, self-esteem, and personal goals

Family Therapy - examining the family as a unit, its value system, and its relationships in order to assess the family's contribution to the problem and decide if

changes are needed to accommodate a recovering
abuser

Aftercare - providing for follow-up support after treatment ends

Keep these components in mind when you consider a
recovery resource because there is a variety of treatment
approaches. They range from weekly sessions with an
individual counselor to a full-blown residential treatment
center requiring a stay of months. Nobody has cornered
the market on the successful treatment of abusing teenagers, and nobody claims a very high success rate. It is a
difficult business and not a very precise one. The needs of
the clients are just as different as the approaches that can
be taken; matching the two is a bit of a guessing game.
Following are very general descriptions of some approaches to recovery.

INDIVIDUAL COUNSELING

Families often prefer to use resources that they already
know. Such resources may include the family doctor, a
school counselor or social worker, or a mental health
resource person such as a psychologist or a psychiatrist.
These professionals will be most effective if they have
proper training and experience in dependency counseling.
A professional with fewer academic degrees but greater
experience and training may be a better choice than a
high-status professional who doesn't specialize in dependency treatment.

GROUP SESSIONS

Sometimes sponsored by community agencies or schools, these meetings allow kids to gather to discuss their common problems of abuse. Usually a trained counselor is present to guide the discussions and keep the group focused on task.

ALCOHOLICS ANONYMOUS

This organization is for teenagers with drug or alcohol problems as well as for adults. In the field of recovery it's safe to say that the AA model is the most respected and most imitated. It is not successful every time but has been a godsend for millions of recovering abusers.

An example is the student who was ordered by a juvenile judge to attend AA meetings for a year and get signed verification at each meeting. At first he grumbled and grouched, but as time wore on and he came to understand the process, he also became a part of it. With the help of the group, sobriety gradually won him over. The process doesn't always take hold so dramatically, but it is a very powerful resource which is available to anyone and everyone.

OUTPATIENT FACILITIES

Recovery facilities once operated on a nonprofit basis, supported by different levels of government or by charitable contributions. Now there are organizations that are in the business of treating dependency and hope to make a profit. One kind is not necessarily better than the other. Recently hospitals have begun to set up programs for the chemically dependent; they have the proper facilities, a staff already in place, and experience in setting up healing programs. Some have developed exemplary programs. Outpatient programs usually require a patient to spend three to eight hours per day in the facility and the remaining time at school or at home. Sometimes the programs add an educational component so that students don't lose too much academic ground at their home school. The biggest disadvantage to the outpatient approach is that the program loses control of the client when he or she is off the grounds. That drawback is somewhat offset if the program requires periodic tests to detect drugs or alcohol in the system. Another consideration is the very practical one of lower costs when compared to full residential treatment.

RESIDENTIAL TREATMENT FACILITIES

Besides including an educational component, these facilities offer the special advantages of around-the-clock control and surveillance, a total separation from the former environment, and enough time for full-scale treatment.

Normally there is an intake process that uses interviews, surveys, and tests for a psychological workup. Counselors use the information from this workup to initiate treatment. Besides individual sessions with staff members such as dependency counselors, psychologists, or psychiatrists, treatment often includes role playing, life scripting, family counseling, and group sessions with other adolescents.

Full-blown treatment is like a rebuilding process; it is not easy for youngsters to abandon both their former behavior and their former image as abusers. Assuming a new "straight" identity is traumatic and compounds the normal insecurities of youth by unraveling the old personality and building a new one, creating a brand new image. Kids often feel as if they must start over from the very beginning.

MAKING THE MATCH

The final choice of a resource requires that you match your child with an appropriate treatment approach. An essential step is to talk to the people in your community who make the referrals—usually social workers, chemical dependency counselors, school counselors, or the local government agency that keeps tabs on recovery resources. Those who make the actual referrals soon get a feel for the approach and style of each resource and receive valuable feedback from clients and their families.

You also may want to accept input from your youngster. Sometimes the teenage grapevine has the inside information on treatment quality; if a particular facility has a strong reputation, and your child has confidence in it, that might be your best choice. Don't rely on that input alone, however, because a youngster who doesn't have a sincere commitment to recovery may lobby for the easiest and most convenient program rather than the most effective.

Like all organizations, the skill of the employees is the most important ingredient in any drug treatment program.

Often ex-abusers are key employees because their personal histories qualify them in a special way. They can establish rapport with skeptical youngsters who can't believe that anyone else can possibly understand what they are going through. Ex-abusers not only can "talk the talk" but they have "walked the walk." That factor alone gives them high credibility.

You probably will be limited to resources that are convenient in your area and that fit the family budget. Health insurance plans very widely in their willingness to pay for recovery programs, so check your insurance coverage first.

REENTRY

Most ex-abusers describe themselves as recovering—not recovered. They are reluctant to claim victory over dependency because they know that they must win the battle every day, one day at a time. Kids returning from treatment simultaneously return to their former life—the same family, same friends, and the same environment. These are the exact conditions that provided the seedbed in which chemical abuse started to grow.

It requires strength of character to stay with the program. Unless a program has prepared the youngster well, there's a very good chance of instant replay. Essential to recovery is a structured follow-up plan that lends support and continuing insight into the entire recovery process. There must be regular meetings with a counselor or other recovering abusers. Going it alone is an unnecessary hardship; in fact, when kids spurn aftercare programs, it often means that resuming their old ways interests them more than recovery.

Insist on a solid aftercare program.

RELOADING

You will be tested to your farthest limits if your youngster completes treatment and then returns home only to resume the same destructive habits. But you must remember that treatment hasn't necessarily failed because it didn't shut down abuse completely; there is a delayed reaction which veterans call "spitting in the soup." This untidy term means that once treatment has forced a client to confront his abuse and acknowledge its effects on his life, abuse takes on another taste. It isn't such carefree, irresponsible fun anymore. Once you know that you are hurting others as well as yourself, the satisfaction drops dramatically.

That's why you must be willing to consider a second treatment attempt if conditions seem ripe. The residue from the initial treatment often provides a running start on a second attempt, the one that could be the turning point.

Chapter Eleven

Silver Lining Department

This book begins with what must be done to protect kids from experimentation and concludes with the serious problems of living with a determined abuser. The point is that the progression need not begin and, if it does, it need not be inevitable. The hope is that you will have the knowledge and tenacity to do battle each step of the way. If you do, you can hold up your head as a parent and be confident that you have done your best. Giving up is the worst mistake. Even when things are blackest there is plenty of reason for optimism, although it is very difficult to put a long-range perspective on a problem while it is threatening to dominate your life.

The first step is to let go of the responsibility you probably feel for the problem. Many of us are programmed to blame ourselves when our children fall short; it seems to go with the territory. Some parents continue to feel responsible for their children even after they themselves have become grandparents. One way to ease those feelings of responsibility is to be in contact with parents in the same boat. Parent support groups are a good resource, as is an organization such as ALANON, a branch of AA geared exclusively for family members of abusers.

From this support you'll learn that you have not failed personally, but that you, too, have become victimized by abuse. You will learn firsthand the healing power of sharing your story with those who can understand; and you will, in turn, listen with understanding as others share their stories. You'll learn how to stand ready to help when the time comes.

A second step is to remember that the despair that you feel seldom lasts forever. Kids do grow out of their youthful habits, and they also can grow out of chemical abuse habits, especially if they never reach a serious stage of dependency. Following are some examples of factors that can cause young people to give up abuse.

MOTORCYCLE SYNDROME

Youth is a time for risk taking. For example, kids love the exhilaration of driving fast and recklessly on motorcycles, but they seldom continue into adulthood. As they age and see a bit more of life, they lose their sense of immortality. They begin to settle into a life-style emphasizing less danger and more self-preservation. Similarly, going out to see how drunk you can get or how long you can stay high are youthful, immature acts. Kids grow out of that stage and move on to saner ways of meeting their personal needs. Time is on your side as your children mature.

THE HEART ATTACK

The heart attack we're talking about is love, as in romance. Many a youngster who loves his parents, but not enough to stop using, has turned around because of the love of another young person. When the stakes are high enough, as when a loving relationship might end because of abuse, chemicals can lose their priority instantly. That's why it may be wise to include boy- or girlfriends in an intervention. But this works only if the relationship is sound and the other youngster is mature enough to understand the process.

One family had this experience. During college their son smoked marijuana occasionally and admitted it. No amount of persuasion or argument could budge him from what he thought was his right to smoke it if he chose. His parents were upset but had very little leverage. They expressed surprise when they learned from him offhandedly during his senior year that he had stopped smoking pot six months ago. The reason: "Ginny doesn't like it." Case closed.

A CHANGED ENVIRONMENT

During the Viet Nam conflict many soldiers became dependent on heroin, a potent drug that produces both physical and psychological dependency. There was great concern that these men would return and be unable to give up their dependent behavior. But the Veterans Administration found that 88 percent of these men were able to give up the dependency once they returned home to a completely different life situation. From combat in

Vietnam to civilian life in the United States is admittedly an extreme example of a change in environment, but it underscores the fact that environment affects dependency.

The environment of Vietnam was different not only geographically but also psychologically. Changing the psychological environment can make an enormous difference. The pressures of adolescence can't be compared to the pressures of the battlefield, but adolescent stress is a real crisis for many youngsters. Once they have passed through adolescence, with its many opportunities for comparison and competition, many of those pressures dissipate. A major environmental change always occurs when children move out on their own, especially when the move forces them to be financially independent. Job responsibility becomes more serious. Often a decent job uncovers stability and dependability in youngsters that they never showed in the past. Succeeding on the job can do wonders for self-esteem.

Choosing to squander money on drugs and alcohol isn't so easy when rent, food, clothing, and insurance are competing for a slice of the budget. Financial independence can change priorities fast.

THE MESSAGE YOU SEND

Many, many youngsters in treatment feel strongly that their parents don't care about them. They are resentful because they never believed that their parents tried very hard to stop them. The classic picture they paint is one of parents who erupt in occasional outbursts of anger and threats but never follow up. The eruptions fade into long periods of indifference and neglect.

While you are impatiently waiting for your child to see the light, it is reassuring to know that by battling every step of the way, you have made it clear that you care too much to abandon your child to abuse. Even at their most belligerent and defiant moments, youngsters know in their hearts that you are doing the right thing and doing it for their sake.

THE UNLOCKED DOOR

No matter how tough you must be in your campaign to free your children from dependency, don't ever close the door and write them off. When a user has sunk deep into dependency, the only life preserver left may be the deep-down belief that, in a crunch, the family will help. As the old saying goes, "Home is the place where, when you go there, they have to let you in."

An open door means that you will always listen but only agree to help when the commitment is real and sincere. It doesn't mean that you should provide a comfortable place to regroup for the next binge. Knowing the difference between a commitment and just another con job is not easy. But if you insist on action, such as entering treatment or attending recovery sessions, you can safely offer support as long as there is proof of sobriety.

Make the abuser realize that the door is always unlocked, but it can be opened only by a commitment to change.

CULTURAL STIRRINGS

Twenty years ago who would have believed that smoking tobacco would become a public issue with laws passed to protect nonsmokers? People have decided that they are no longer willing to inhale unhealthy fumes from another's cigarette. The health issue has changed the public's perception of cigarette smoking. As a result, tobacco is in a serious sales decline. The health issue for drugs and alcohol is different, but the public seems to be changing how it perceives teenage abuse as well.

The two areas that are surfacing and drawing attention are teenage automobile fatalities and teenage suicides. The carnage from auto accidents spawned an organization called *Mothers Against Drunk Driving* (MADD), which will surely have a nationwide effect on teenage drinking. There is also a growing national organization called *Students Against Drunk Driving* (SADD). The annual increase in teenage suicides, over half of which involve drugs or alcohol, has focused attention on both adolescent stress and teenage abuse. As parents become aware and concerned, they will be more alert to these problems. They will take more preventive actions in their homes and add support to the community and national movements that are underway.

Even the alcohol industry has shifted some of its advertising emphasis to such subjects as the importance of limiting intake and the importance of designating a nondrinking driver. This may reflect the industry's guilty conscience for marketing such a destructive substance, but it also may be a reaction to the public's unhappy awareness of that destruction. It is clearly an admission by alcohol producers that they are selling a dangerous product. Some communities now are offering free taxi rides home for those who are too drunk to drive on holidays like New Year's Eve. These defensive tactics serve as reminders to us all that alcoholic abuse does kill people, including teenagers. Hopefully, these reminders will contribute to a decline in alcohol use by young people.

A NEW EDUCATIONAL DIRECTION

Movements and campaigns designed to protect youngsters from abuse are rapidly springing up. They include more than simply educating kids to the dangers of addiction. The new thrust is focusing on abstinence as a positive step, as an achievement, and as a life-enhancing choice rather than a choice grounded in fear. A most encouraging sign is the movement in schools encouraging kids to say NO to drugs. The National Football League is reinforcing this tactic by sending professional players into schools to talk to students about making the right decisions.

There will always be teenagers who try to gain status by doing the forbidden, acting in defiance of the establishment. But as more kids make public their commitment to stay clean, the status for using diminishes as the peer pressure to abstain becomes a stronger and more positive force.

WE can win the battle against teenage abuse; WE can win as a nation and YOU can win as a parent. We hope this book will help.

Chapter Twelve

Superquick Summary

1. Remember that every child is a candidate for chemical abuse, especially an uninformed child.

2. Don't underestimate the many powerful forces that encourage teenagers to use alcohol and illegal drugs. You must neutralize these forces.

3. The position you take and the example you set are the two most influential factors in the choices your children make.

4. YOU must teach your kids to say NO; don't rely on others.

5. Trust your children, but never relax your vigilance.

6. Be familiar with warning signs.

7. When you become uneasy, worried, or confused, check it out with someone experienced in teenage chemical abuse.

8. If suspicions mount, use low-key confrontation.

9. If you discover experimentation:

   a. plan your approach in unity with your spouse.
   b. let the emotions dissipate first, then arrange a calm disclosure session.
   c. encourage an abstinence pledge.
   d. remain vigilant but don't harass.

10. If use continues:

    a. arrange a professional evaluation.
    b. use the *Dependency Quiz*.
    c. put the pressure on for a signed contract.
    d. suggest counseling or a support group.

11. If abuse becomes entrenched:

    a. arrange counseling or a support group for other family members.
    b. check out 'enabling' behavior by family members.
    c. arrange a professional intervention.
    d. raise the bottom.
    e. argue hard for treatment.
    f. remove the abuser from the household.

13. Teenage use or abuse doesn't mean certain destruction. Maturity, falling in love, or a changed environment are just some of the circumstances in life that can cause a turn-around. Time is on your side if you never give up.

14. Teenage abuse can be attacked; momentum is growing in our society to end the carnage. You, as a parent, are the key. Promise yourself to do your very best.

Glossary

abuse, abuser - using alcohol or drugs to the extent that life is affected adversely

Acapulco gold - high potency marijuana grown in Mexico

acid - slang for a family of drugs, including LSD, that produce hallucinations

addiction - an overwhelming, irresistible craving for a substance

aftercare - continuing treatment and/or monitoring after completing a treatment program

amphetamines - synthetic amines which act as stimulants - benzedrine, methedrine, and so on

angel dust - a drug in powdered form, often mixed with marijuana or other hallucinogens

bad trip - a panicky reaction to a hallucinogen

bang - an ingestion of narcotics

barbiturates - a group of drugs that depress the nervous system - amytol, nembutal, seconal, and so on

bennies - benzedrine pills

bag - nickel bag, dime bag, big bag; used to describe quantities of drugs

blow your mind - an extreme high, often losing control

bombed - intoxicated or 'out of it' from drugs or alcohol

bust, busted - an arrest or being caught by any authority figure

chip - to take drugs irregularly in low quantities

cocaine, coke - a drug extracted from the leaves of the coca bush; it produces a quick euphoria and the illusion of strength, endurance, and heightened mental capacity

cold turkey - abrupt, complete withdrawal from narcotics

Columbian - high grade marijuana from Columbia

connection - a source for drugs

crack - a derivative of cocaine in the form of rock-like crystals, often smoked

crash - to collapse and/or sleep after a prolonged drug experience

cross-tolerance - tolerance developed to one drug transferred to another - the reactions are the same

cut - to dilute a drug with another substance

deal, dealer - to traffic in illegal narcotics

denial - unwilling to admit, even to oneself, the true extent of use or abuse

dependency - the condition reached when a person is unable to stop using a substance

dope - any illegal narcotic

downer - a depressant drug that relaxes and tranquilizes

druggies - consistent users of drugs, usually used derisively

evaluation - an objective opinion of the extent of use/-abuse by an experienced person

fix - a dose of drugs

flip out - a temporary psychotic reaction to a drug

glue sniffing - inhaling the fumes from glue to get high

grass - marijuana

goofball - any pill that makes one act 'goofy'

hash, hashish - a resin from the hemp plant, *cannabis sativa*

heroin - a powerful derivative of morphine which produces a relaxed euphoria; highly addictive - also called H, horse, junk

high - a drug-induced state of euphoria

hit - a dose or quantity of a substance

hooked - being chemically dependent

hold, holding - having illegal substances in possession

joint - a marijuana cigarette

junkie - a person dependent and messed up by drugs

marijuana - the name for parts of hemp plants, can be smoked or ingested to reach a 'high'

methadone - a synthetic opiate used to maintain addicts who are off other drugs - in itself addictive

minimizing - downgrading the true extent of use or abuse

morphine - derived from opium; less potent than heroin but addictive as well

opium - made from the seeds of a poppy; a pain reliever and sedative, addictive

overdose - too much of a substance producing a coma or death by depressing the nervous system

popping - injecting drugs beneath the skin

pot - marijuana

pot pipe - a device, often made of metal and shaped like a pipe, used to smoke marijuana

pothead - a steady user of marijuana who often appears in a stupor

roach - the butt of a marijuana cigarette, sometimes held with a roach clip to extract the last few puffs

rush - the initial euphoric feeling from the first reaction to a substance

sniffing - inhaling drugs, usually cocaine or heroin powder, thorugh the nostrils

snow - cocaine crystals

speed - uppers, usually pills taken to create or maintain a high

spaced out - out of touch with reality when intoxicated or hallucinating

stash - a hiding place for drugs and equipment or referring to the actual drugs and equipment

toke - a puff from or smoking a marijuana cigarette

user - anyone ingesting alcohol or illegal drugs

upper - amphetamine pills or any substance that produces a rush of good feelings

withdrawal - the reaction to stopping heavy substance use, which is often restlessness, weakness, nausea, trembling, and so on

Suggested Reading

Alibrandi, Tom, *Young Alcoholics*, Minneapolis, MN: CompCare Publications, 1978.

Cohen, Sidney, MD, *The Substance Abuse Problem*, New York: Haworth Press, 1981.

Hatterer, Dr. Lawrence, *The Pleasure Addicts*, South Brunswick, NJ: A.S. Barnes, 1989.

Hodgkinson, Liz, *Addiction*, New York: Thorson's Publishing Group, 1986.

Johnson, Vernon E., *Intervention*, Minneapolis, MN: Johnson Institute Books, 1986.

Lingeman, Richard R., *Drugs From A to Z*, New York: McGraw Hill, 1974.

Mills, James, *The Underground Empire*, Garden City, NJ: Doubleday, 1986.

Mothner, Ira and Weitz Alan, *How To Get Off Drugs*, San Francisco: Rolling Stones Press, 1984.

Mumey, Jack, *Young Alcoholics, A Book for Parents*, Chicago: Contemporary Books, Inc., 1984.

National Institute on Alcohol Abuse, *National Strategy for Prevention of Drug Abuse and Drug Trafficking*, (Gov't. Doc. Ref. NF HE 20.8302:D84/3) Washington, DC: U.S. Government Printing Office, 1984.

Polson, Beth and Newton, Miller, *Not My Kid*, New York: Arbor House, 1984.

Schlaadt, Richard G., *Drugs of Choice*, Englewood Cliffs, NJ: Prentice-Hall, 1982.

Source. Minneapolis, MN.: Search Institute, Spring, 1984 (Quarterly Publication).

Svendsen, Roger, *Chemical Health*, Minneapolis, MN.: The American Lutheran Church, 1986, (Booklet).